WHY THE WAIT, LORD?

LEARNING TO RESPOND TO OUR GOD, WHO IS NEVER IN A HURRY

FIVE-WEEK STUDY

LAURA SIMPSON

WESTBOW
PRESS®
A DIVISION OF THOMAS NELSON
& ZONDERVAN

WestBow Press books may be ordered through booksellers or by contacting:

WestBow Press
A Division of Thomas Nelson & Zondervan
1663 Liberty Drive
Bloomington, IN 47403
www.westbowpress.com
844-714-3454

ISBN: 978-1-6642-2250-2 (sc)
ISBN: 978-1-6642-2249-6 (e)

Library of Congress Control Number: 2021902123

Print information available on the last page.

WestBow Press rev. date: 03/31/2021

CONTENTS

INTRODUCTION

WHY IS IT TAKING SO LONG?

Life is full of waiting, and few, if any of us, are fond of it. We despise having to be patient in a doctor's waiting room. We demand that our food be ready in less than three minutes. Sometimes two-day shipping is just not quick enough.

We have places to go, people to see, and things to do. If we do not accomplish 110 percent of our to-do list in the first half of the day, we feel like we are wasting time, missing out on something, or doing something wrong. In a world where communication is instant, thoughts and opinions are expressed before the art of articulation has a chance to work. When responses are expected within the hour, waiting feels like a cruel and unusual punishment. Yet God often works in seasons of waiting.

At the time of writing this study, I am thirty-three years old, over a decade into my career, and single with no kids. My deep desires have been left unfulfilled. All I ever wanted to be in life was a wife and mother.

Granted, I have thoroughly enjoyed my singleness because of the opportunities that I am able to partake in *because* I am single. I refuse to waste a second of my singleness. However, nothing has taken away the guttural voice that says, *I was made to be a great wife and mom*. Why hasn't it happened yet? Why are so many of my friends and I still waiting to get married?

I knew that I needed to plant myself firmly in the Word. I needed to get to know others who knew God in a way that I desperately want to know Him. I had to remind myself that the women whom we are about to study together weren't just characters but real people. I wanted a toolbox and actual examples of how to wait well in a practical way. I invite you to get to know these amazing women as well and change the way you respond to the uncomfortable times of waiting that we want to skip. What if God actually does something greater in the unseen and seemingly silent times of our lives? What if it is deeper than our desires for on-time appointments and quick, hot food? What if far more intense issues, which consume the mind and heart, lie there?

This study is meant to cause you to take a step back and see that seasons of waiting are often when God is doing His greatest work. Spiritual blessings are not only bestowed on the individual but to others as well when we trust that God has ordained these seasons for our good. Make no mistake; it will be a journey. If the questions seem too hard and deep, I implore you to dig deeper. Don't just answer yes or no.

There is no space that Jesus has left untouched. He will guide your heart and handle it very carefully. Trust Him with these next five weeks and ask Him to reveal Himself and His heart to you. If you give God the time, I promise that He will reward your seeking by revealing more of His heart to you. You are going to wait regardless, so why not let God show you what He has for you in it?

BEFORE YOU START

Over the next five weeks, we are going to look at six women who faced similar dilemmas that you and I deal with today. Through their responses, we'll learn the spiritual benefits that come from seasons of waiting.

During the week, you will read a primary text each day. I encourage you to read it in the different translations that have been provided. For example on Day 1, use the Bible that you do most of your studying in (probably ESV or NIV). Then on every other day, read the different translations that have been provided for you. I have found that this helps me not get so comfortable with the text that I miss things. Different versions are provided so that you can compare them, mark them up, and make notes in them. You'll remember a lot more if you write it down. However, if that seems overwhelming, just stick to your own Bible.

Each day will end with a time of prayer. Sometimes the prayers will be written out, and at other times, there will be space for you to write your own. In a few days of the study, there is a time to speak prayers aloud or in your heart. The importance does not lie in the way that you wish to communicate with God but in doing it. In a study about time and waiting, prayer is truly the key component. Wait for the Lord. See what He stirs in your heart and wants to say.

My prayer for this study and you is that as you find the strength to walk through seasons you would rather avoid and certainly wouldn't pick for yourself, Jesus will meet you in your most intimate and sacred space. I pray that your heart will be open and that these pages will somehow reveal the things that God loves to do in our times of waiting. Most of all, I pray that you will fall more in love with our God and respond to waiting differently than you have.

WEEK 1

SARAH

Waiting in the Midst of the Impossible

What circumstance in your world seems utterly impossible because it's not only an ever-enduring longing and deep desire but also because it seems to defy the laws of science and reality? You don't even talk to your closest friend about it because you don't want to hear the practical words that you know are true: "It's impossible." It would be like starting out on a remote island, swimming across the ocean, biking to Mount Everest, climbing to the top and taking a selfie in a day— it's physically impossible.

Now, I know that you may be thinking, *We're really studying Sarah? She's not exactly the person that I would call the ideal example of how to wait properly.* You'd be correct in thinking that. She got scared and impatient. She meddled a bit. However, she also gets a bad rap. Sarah ended up in the well-known Hall of Faith, which is found in Hebrews. We can learn plenty from her experience. We have all become impatient, been scared, and taken matters into our own hands. God's faithfulness to us in these times is a great grace. Hebrews 11:11 says these beautiful words about her.

> Sarah's faith embraced the miracle power to conceive even though she was barren and was past the age of childbearing, for the authority of her faith rested in the One who made the promise, and *she tapped into his faithfulness.* (The Passion Translation [TPT]; emphasis mine)

Sarah had an interesting relationship with hope. This week, we will learn what it looks like to live out a desperate hope that we feel we need to control and a trusting hope that allows God to bring about a result that is beyond our comprehension.

DAY 1

HOPE UNDEFINED

Ask the Holy Spirit to give you ears to hear, eyes to see, and a heart that is open to His Word. Read Genesis 12:2–3, 15:1–5, 16:1–6, and 17:15–19, 21 in your own Bible.

Sarai, lovingly known as Sarah, probably felt a lot of hope and excitement when she was included in the promise that God had given to her husband, Abram, better known as Abraham (see Genesis 15). Even though Sarai was old and barren, Abram was promised a son, not just any son, but a son who would be the heir to God's covenant.

Let's look at how her story unfolds. Sarai was Abram's faithful wife when God called him to leave their home and embark on the journey that God had placed before them, which included an incredible covenantal promise from the Lord. Fill in the blanks below.

> I will make you into a _____, and I will bless you; I will make your
> _____, and you will be a _____. I will bless those who bless
> you, and whoever curses you I will curse; and all peoples on earth will be blessed
> through you. (Genesis 12:2–3)

God would make them into a great nation, a great name, and a great blessing.

Sarai was faithful. She followed her husband. She left everything that she knew and trusted in God. He was the God of promise and results.

While Sarai knew that there would be a great nation, God left out many details of how it would come to pass. It would make sense that because she was Abram's wife, she would be the one to start this great nation. Yet time was passing, and she had not yet given birth to a baby. Hope was giving way to fear and disappointment.

Don't we feel as if God does this to us as well? He gives us just a taste of a promise. While we know we can trust it, He does not spell out every decision and detail of how His timing will work out. The more time marches on, the more our mortal and finite minds believe that His plan isn't going to happen.

We have to wait for God to reveal more of Himself and His plan.

When have you experienced this? Have you ever felt that God spoke to you or included you in a promise of something great that was coming, yet the timing and circumstances didn't match up?

_____

_____

_____

_____

Look back to the last paragraph in the introduction for this week. Most often, do you operate out of desperate hope or trusting hope?

_____

_____

_____

_____

Since we are focusing on waiting while in the midst of the impossible and the way that hope plays into that, what is your knee-jerk reaction when you have hope that something will happen but have no idea how it will play out?

_____

_____

_____

_____

Take time to ask God for courage so that you can continue to walk in faithfulness and believe that He will honor His word to you.

Here is one of the different translations that are provided so that you can read a passage in a new way. If it's a bit overwhelming, stay the course with the Bible that you normally use when studying.

New American Standard Bible (NASB)

And I will make you a great nation, And I will bless you, And make your name great; And so you shall be a blessing; And I will bless those who bless you, And the one who curses you I will curse. And in you all the families of the earth will be blessed.

After these things the word of the Lord came to Abram in a vision, saying, "Do not fear, Abram, I am a shield to you; Your reward shall be very great." Abram said, "O Lord God, what will You give me, since I am childless, and the heir of my house is Eliezer of Damascus?" And Abram said, "Since You have given no offspring to me, one born in my house is my heir." Then behold, the word of the Lord came to him, saying, "This man will not be your heir; but one who will come forth from your own body, he shall be your heir." And He took him outside and said, "Now look toward the heavens, and count the stars, if you are able to count them." And He said to him, "So shall your descendants be."

Now Sarai, Abram's wife had borne him no children, and she had an Egyptian maid whose name was Hagar. So Sarai said to Abram, "Now behold, the Lord has prevented me from bearing children. Please go in to my maid; perhaps I will obtain children through her." And Abram listened to the voice of Sarai. After Abram had lived ten years in the land of Canaan, Abram's wife Sarai took Hagar the Egyptian, her maid, and gave her to her husband Abram as his wife. He went in to Hagar, and she conceived; and when she saw that she had conceived, her mistress was despised in her sight. And Sarai said to Abram, "May the wrong done me be upon you. I gave my maid into your arms, but when she saw that she had conceived, I was despised in her sight. May the Lord judge between you and me." But Abram said to Sarai, "Behold, your maid is in your power; do to her what is good in your sight." So Sarai treated her harshly, and she fled from her presence.

Then God said to Abraham, "As for Sarai your wife, you shall not call her name Sarai, but Sarah shall be her name. I will bless her, and indeed I will give you a son by her. Then I will bless her, and she shall be a mother of nations; kings of peoples will come from her." Then Abraham fell on his face and laughed, and said in his heart, "Will a child be born to a man one hundred years old? And will Sarah, who is ninety years old, bear a child?" And Abraham said to God, "Oh that Ishmael might live before You!" But God said, "No, but Sarah your wife will bear you a son, and you shall call his name Isaac; and I will establish My covenant with him for an everlasting covenant for his descendants after him. … But My covenant I will establish with Isaac, whom Sarah will bear to you at this season next year." (Genesis 12:2–3; 15:1–5; 16:1–6; 17:15–19, 21)

DAY 2

HOPE DEFERRED

Ask the Holy Spirit to give you ears to hear, eyes to see, and a heart that is open to His Word. Read Genesis 12:2–3, 15:1–5, 16:1–6, and 17:15–19, 21 in the text provided on the previous page.

Between Genesis 12 and 15, time passed, and Sarai's hope that this child would come through her also passed. But the Lord had not forgotten Sarai. Again, read what happens in chapter 15.

What does Abraham ask God?

_____

_____

_____

_____

How does the Lord answer him (verse 4)?

_____

_____

_____

_____

Some would say that Sarai's waiting started when she heard the news that she would bear a son and then failed to get pregnant right away. She actually would have been waiting all her life. When she was a little girl, she would have waited to get married. Once she was married, she would have waited until she was pregnant. Once she was pregnant, she would have waited for the child to develop and grow before she could give birth, and so on.

In the gap between the promise and the fulfillment
of the promise, her waiting intensified.

Sarai seemed to be thwarted in phase two. She was unable to conceive. During every month that had passed, her hope had shattered as her body had denied her the very thing that she had desired for so long. Maybe she longed for the day that her body would be well past the childbearing years. Maybe she hoped the desire to be a mother would subside and that there would no longer be a constant reminder of what she would never have the opportunity to be. However, in her season of waiting when she tried to kill all hope and accept the terms of her body, the prospect of it coming to pass could have ignited a flame of hope again.[1]

Record a situation in your life that feels as if the waiting has become intensified.

_____

_____

_____

_____

In that intensity, do you have thoughts of being thwarted?

_____

_____

_____

_____

While in your secret place and even though you have accepted the terms, is there a tiny part of you that hopes God can do the impossible and that He wants to work in your circumstance? If so, where is that hope coming from?

_____

_____

_____

_____

Read Hebrews 11:1 and 2 Corinthians 4:18. Remind yourself where your true hope lies.

_____

_____

_____

_____

God of miracles,

I praise You today. I thank You that while You allow reality, You also call us to hope in the One who is greater. You have said that I have not because I ask not, so, God, I place my request for the impossible before You. Your granting of my request does not determine whether You are good or not. You will always remain good, Father, but I ask You to meet me in this place and hear my heart's cry. Regardless of the outcome, I trust that You will give me what is best for me. Help me to trust You more.

New Living Translation (NLT)

I will make you into a great nation. I will bless you and make you famous, and you will be a blessing to others. I will bless those who bless you and curse those who treat you with contempt. All the families on earth will be blessed through you.

Some time later, the Lord spoke to Abram in a vision and said to him, "Do not be afraid, Abram, for I will protect you, and your reward will be great." But Abram replied, "O Sovereign Lord, what good are all your blessings when I don't even have a son? Since you've given me no children, Eliezer of Damascus, a servant in my household, will inherit all my wealth. You have given me no descendants of my own, so one of my servants will be my heir." Then the Lord said to him, "No, your servant will not be your heir, for you will have a son of your own who will be your heir." Then the Lord took Abram outside and said to him, "Look up into the sky and count the stars if you can. That's how many descendants you will have!"

Now Sarai, Abram's wife, had not been able to bear children for him. But she had an Egyptian servant named Hagar. So Sarai said to Abram, "The Lord has prevented me from having children. Go and sleep with my servant. Perhaps I can have children through her." And Abram agreed with Sarai's proposal. So Sarai, Abram's wife, took Hagar the Egyptian servant and gave her to Abram as a wife. (This happened ten years after Abram had settled in the land of Canaan.) So Abram had sexual relations with Hagar, and she became pregnant. But when Hagar knew she was pregnant, she began to treat her mistress, Sarai, with contempt. Then Sarai said to Abram, "This is all your fault! I put my servant into your arms, but now that she's pregnant she treats me with contempt. The Lord will show who's wrong—you or me!" Abram replied, "Look, she is your servant, so deal with her as you see fit." Then Sarai treated Hagar so harshly that she finally ran away.

Then God said to Abraham, "Regarding Sarai, your wife—her name will no longer be Sarai.

From now on her name will be Sarah. And I will bless her and give you a son from her! Yes, I will bless her richly, and she will become the mother of many nations. Kings of nations will be among her descendants." Then Abraham bowed down to the ground, but he laughed to himself in disbelief. "How could I become a father at the age of 100?" he thought. "And how can Sarah have a baby when she is ninety years old?" So Abraham said to God, "May Ishmael live under your special blessing!" But God replied, "No—Sarah, your wife, will give birth to a son for you. You will name him Isaac, and I will confirm my covenant with him and his descendants as an everlasting covenant. But my covenant will be confirmed with Isaac, who will be born to you and Sarah about this time next year." (Genesis 12:2–3; 15:1–5; 16:1–6; 17:15–19, 21)

DAY 3

HOPE UNDONE

Ask the Holy Spirit to give you ears to hear, eyes to see, and a heart that is open to His Word. Read Genesis 12:2–3, 15:1–5, 16:1–6, 17:15–19, 21 in the text provided. Focus on Genesis 16:1–6.

Sarah was included in the promise to her husband, but no baby had come yet. What did Sarai do as she waited for the impossible?

_____

_____

_____

_____

She concluded that God needed her help. She tried to force a result. She wanted the promise to be fulfilled.

Abram was seventy-five years old when God gave him the promise of an heir (Sarai was sixty-five years old; see Genesis 12:1–4). He was ninety when God confirmed the covenant promise (Sarai was eighty).

She could not believe that God would or could do the impossible of allowing her to carry a child in her old, barren, and worn-out body. The idea of handing over someone else to sleep with your own husband strikes us as horrific on all accounts. This was a culturally acceptable practice, but it circumvented the promise of God and bypassed waiting on His hands to move instead of her own. As one commentator explained,

"Possibly their mistake is seeing the promise of God not as a privilege, but as an obligation. Instead of saying, 'We're going to have a baby!' they say, 'We've got to have a baby!' And whenever one sees the fruit of God's promises as something to be achieved rather than received, all sorts of options present themselves."[2]

In what ways have you tried to manipulate a situation to reach the result that God has promised? Have you ever tried to help God out by using what seemed like a good or reasonable option instead of waiting on God?

_____

_____

_____

_____

Referencing the commentator's quote, why do we think it's easier to look at the promise from God as an obligation rather than a privilege?

_____

_____

_____

_____

Looking again at the last paragraph in the introduction, what type of hope was Sarah demonstrating?

_____

_____

_____

_____

Such reasoning gives us the illusion that we are controlling God. If we're honest, we are afraid that He won't actually do what He has promised to do. We are afraid that we might have misheard or that we did not see the promise correctly, thereby risking being hurt, disappointed, and possibly looking a bit absurd to those around us.

So in order to not make God look bad, we *have* to make it happen. However, our timing is not God's timing. If God initiated the promise (He truly initiated it, and it was not something you obligated God to do), you can be sure that He will remain true to His Word.[3]

If you have access, look up Psalm 27:14 in the Passion Translation as a commentary on the verse that states "Wait on the Lord; be strong and take heart and wait on the Lord." Record it below.

_____

_____

_____

_____

Sarai struggled with impatience. As is often the case when manipulation produces the intended result, Hagar discovered that she was with child and came to despise Sarai. The relationship between Sarai and Hagar was disrupted. She called for Abram to take responsibility for the family and keep the peace.[4] Yet Abram refused to own his responsibility and left Hagar in the hands of Sarai.

How did Sarah treat Hagar?

_____

_____

_____

_____

Because of her own frustration with the entire situation, she treated Hagar in such a harsh manner that Hagar fled. All the while, God was not done with Sarai. In the impossibility of the situation, God was waiting on the right time to fulfill His promise to Abram.

> *Even in her need for control, meddling, and unbelief, God was going to prove Himself faithful. He always does what He says He will do.*

In Genesis 17, God changed their names. Abram became Abraham, which meant the "father of many." Sarai became Sarah, signifying that she would be the mother of many nations.[5]

This was kind of God. He could have just declared the news of Genesis 12:2–3 and stopped there, expecting Abram and Sarai to move forward and trust that He would work everything out. Sometimes God does this with us, and we *can* trust Him.

What does Romans 8:28 tell us?

_____

_____

_____

_____

But God, in His kindness, gave them Genesis 15, which was the marriage to the previous engagement: a covenant.

God didn't stop there. Proceed to Genesis 17:15-16. When He changed their names, what else did He change?

_____

_____

_____

_____

In verse 19, what did God say to Abraham?

_____

_____

_____

_____

Explain the hope that is found in verse 21.

_____

_____

_____

_____

The Abrahamic Covenant is unconditional, meaning that absolutely nothing can thwart the things that God has promised—not a barren womb, advanced age, another child that came before. Abraham was promised to become a great nation, name, and blessing to the world. God would do what He said He would do.

God said these things to Abraham but not to Sarah. Do not let that deter you. Surely, Abraham let Sarah know what the Lord had told him. He must have noted that God had said the child would come through her. It is a beautiful thing when iron can sharpen iron and two believers can encourage each other to keep taking steps forward in faith together.

Take time to thank God for His reassurances of hope. If you know a person who helps sharpen your iron, thank God for him or her too.

The Message (MSG)

I'll make you a great nation and bless you. I'll make you famous; you'll be a blessing. I'll bless those who bless you; those who curse you I'll curse. All the families of the Earth will be blessed through you.

After all these things, this word of God came to Abram in a vision: "Don't be afraid, Abram. I'm your shield. Your reward will be grand!" Abram said, "God, Master, what use are your gifts as long as I'm childless and Eliezer of Damascus is going to inherit everything?" Abram continued, "See, you've given me no children, and now a mere house servant is going to get it all." Then God's Message came: "Don't worry, he won't be your heir; a son from your body will be your heir." Then he took him outside and said, "Look at the sky. Count the stars. Can you do it? Count your descendants! You're going to have a big family, Abram!"

Sarai, Abram's wife, hadn't yet produced a child. She had an Egyptian maid named Hagar. Sarai said to Abram, "God has not seen fit to let me have a child. Sleep with my maid. Maybe I can get a family from her." Abram agreed to do what Sarai said. So Sarai, Abram's wife, took her Egyptian maid Hagar and gave her to her husband Abram as a wife. Abram had been living ten years in Canaan when this took place. He slept with Hagar and she got pregnant. When Hagar learned she was pregnant, she looked down on her mistress. Sarai told Abram, "It's all your fault that I'm suffering this abuse. I put my maid in bed with you and the minute she knows she's pregnant, she treats me like I'm nothing. May God decide which of us is right." "You decide," said Abram. "Your maid is your business." Sarai was abusive to Hagar and Hagar ran away.

God continued speaking to Abraham, "And Sarai your wife: Don't call her Sarai any longer; call her Sarah. I'll bless her—yes! I'll give you a son by her! Oh, how I'll bless her! Nations will come from her; kings of nations will come from her." Abraham fell flat on his face. And then he laughed, thinking, "Can a hundred-year-old man father a son? And can Sarah, at ninety years, have a baby?" Recovering, Abraham said to God, "Oh, keep Ishmael alive and well before you!" But God said, "That's not what I mean. Your wife, Sarah, will have a baby, a son. Name him Isaac (Laughter). I'll establish my covenant with him and his descendants, a covenant that lasts forever. But I'll establish my covenant with Isaac whom Sarah will give you about this time next year." (Genesis 12:2–3; 15:1–5; 16:1–6; 17:15–19, 21)

DAY 4

HOPE ARISES

Ask the Holy Spirit to give you ears to hear, eyes to see, and a heart that is open to His Word. Read Genesis 18:1–15 (This is different from the primary text you've been reading).

The Lord then says, "I will surely return to you about this time next year, and _____ will have a son" (verse 10).

What did Sarah do in response? Why?

_____

_____

_____

_____

Some scholars say that she laughed in contempt while others say that it was unbelief.[6] Can anyone blame her? She was eighty-nine years old.

My favorite explanation regarding the text comes from Allen Ross, when he says,

> When something as incredible as this is declared, the human response is consistent: like Sarah, people are taken off guard, laugh and then out of fear deny that they laughed. But God knows human hearts and that Christians often do stagger at what He says He can do.[7]

Nevertheless, the Lord spoke *her* name. This time, she heard it with her own ears. There was no denying that she would bear this child. There was no need to continue to doubt. There was no need to wonder if giving her maidservant to Abraham had ruined her chance to be a part of the story. Scripture states repeatedly that at the very time God determines to do something, it will be done.

> *Sarah, being almost ninety years old, bears the son of the*
> *promise, Isaac.[8] Our hope lies in His timing.*

Not long ago, I was giving a former coworker an update on my life. Her friend, whom I did not know at all, was with her. The friend listened as I talked about a particular situation and concluded by saying, "I think it's just a timing issue. It's just not the right time."

The stranger looked me straight in the eyes, pointed her finger at me, and with the most beautiful African accent, said, "Do not say it is not the right time. It is God's time. Therefore, it cannot be wrong. God's timing is perfect. Do not say it is not the right time when time belongs to God."

I looked back at her while smiling and said, "Amen." I wasn't at all mad that she had scolded me. I was filled with an unexpected hope because this beautiful woman, who was filled with the Spirit, was not afraid to share the very truth that I needed to hear.

We can place trust in the absolute, unchanging character of our God—the God who is for *us* and allows us to rely on grace rather than on striving to please him.

Before the foundations of the earth, He knew that Sarah would bear a child from her old, barren body. Sarah did not have the privilege of being able to open the New Testament and see her name in black and white.

Read Romans 4:17–25 in the New International Version. Look at verse 17. Paul went out of his way to make sure that we would understand,

> The God who gives life to the _____ and calls things that are not as though they were.

In verse 19, he continued writing about Abraham.

Faced the fact that his body was as good as _____—since he was about 100 years old—and that Sarah's womb was also _____.

Dead, dead, dead—he used some form of the same word three times. One is an adjective, one is a verb, and one is a noun. But did you catch it? God gives life to the dead and not only that, He calls things that are not as though they were. Take a deep breath and read that again.

If you have time, read Hebrews 11.

In regards to faith, Sarah is mentioned as being alongside Abraham. Only one other woman is mentioned in this faithful lineup. As Sarah endured sleepless nights because of her grief over her barrenness and then sleepless nights involving a newborn and feedings, I doubt that she ever thought that thousands of years later, people would be reading about her faithfulness. Because Sarah turned her desperate hope into a trusting hope and Jesus's sacrifice, her faith caused us to be included in the promise of the Abrahamic Covenant and adopted into God's family.

Write out a prayer of thankfulness for God's faithfulness in Sarah's life and throughout history. If you are a child of God, you are included in this story. This is your history as well.

_____

_____

_____

_____

New King James Version (NKJV)

I will make you a great nation; I will bless you And make your name great; And you shall be a blessing. I will bless those who bless you, And I will curse him who curses you; And in you all the families of the earth shall be blessed.

After these things the word of the Lord came to Abram in a vision, saying, "Do not be afraid, Abram. I am your shield, your exceedingly great reward." But Abram said, "Lord God, what will You give me, seeing I go childless, and the heir of my house is Eliezer of Damascus?" Then Abram said, "Look, You have given me no offspring; indeed one born in my house is my heir!" And behold, the word of the Lord came to him, saying, "This one shall not be your heir, but one who will come from your own body shall be your heir." Then He brought him outside and said, "Look now toward heaven, and count the stars if you are able to number them." And He said to him, "So shall your descendants be."

Now Sarai, Abram's wife, had borne him no children. And she had an Egyptian maidservant whose name was Hagar. So Sarai said to Abram, "See now, the Lord has restrained me from bearing children. Please, go in to my maid; perhaps I shall obtain children by her." And Abram heeded the voice of Sarai. Then Sarai, Abram's wife, took Hagar her maid, the Egyptian, and gave her to her husband Abram to be his wife, after Abram had dwelt ten years in the land of Canaan. So he went in to Hagar, and she conceived. And when she saw that she had conceived, her mistress became despised in her eyes. Then Sarai said to Abram, "My wrong be upon you! I gave my maid into your embrace; and when she saw that she had conceived, I became despised in her eyes. The Lord judge between you and me." So Abram said to Sarai, "Indeed your maid is in your hand; do to her as you please." And when Sarai dealt harshly with her, she fled from her presence. Then God said to Abraham, "As for Sarai your wife, you shall not call her name Sarai, but Sarah shall be her name. And I will bless her and also give you a son by her; then I will bless her, and she shall be a mother of nations; kings of peoples shall be from her." Then Abraham fell on his face and laughed, and said in his heart, "Shall a child be born to a man who is one hundred years old? And shall Sarah, who is ninety years old, bear a child?" And Abraham said to God, "Oh, that Ishmael might live before You!" Then God said: "No, Sarah your wife shall bear you a son, and you shall call his name Isaac; I will establish My covenant with him for an everlasting covenant, and with his descendants after him. But My covenant I will establish with Isaac, whom Sarah shall bear to you at this set time next year." (Genesis 12:2–3; 15:1–5; 16:1–6; 17:15–19, 21)

DAY 5

HOPE FULFILLED

Ask the Holy Spirit to give you ears to hear, eyes to see, and a heart that is open to His Word. Read Genesis 15:1–5, 17:15–19 and 21, 18:9–15, and 21:1–6 in the text provided.

What did God do in those twenty-five years of intense waiting? He deepened Sarah's faith in Himself, the One True God. He proved Himself faithful time and again. He provided for her. He brought her to a place of dependence on Him through an impossible promise, thereby showing her how faithful He was to His own word.

Is anything too hard for the Lord?

> Sarah said, "God has brought me laughter, and everyone who hears about this will laugh with me." (Genesis 21:1–6)

Circle above the things that God did and underline Sarah's response.

If He followed through on His promise, was there any reason that Sarah should doubt Him? No, but she did and forced her own hand. She went with the best advice that she had been given, and she participated in a practice that was acceptable to her culture. She gave her maidservant to her husband to produce an heir.[2]

Today, major repercussions from this choice have wreaked havoc across the Middle East and have disrupted the whole world. Even though she did what she thought she had to do to bring about the promise, in His grace, God did not remove her role in the promise. She was to be the recipient of an impossible promise and the mother who birthed an entire nation.

When Isaac was born, Sarah praised God because her God was able to fulfill the word that He had promised her. The spiritual benefit of Sarah's situation is our believing that in the face of impossibility, nothing is impossible for God. Therefore, we can hold onto the promise and fully know that God will do what He says He will do.

Read Proverbs 13:12. What does it say about hope deferred?

_____

_____

_____

_____

What does it tell us about hope fulfilled?

_____

_____

_____

_____

Isn't that amazing? Look at all the life that came through Sarah's fulfilled hope throughout the generations. We are a product of her hope and faith!

Now, I'm not advocating that we should ignore the facts. This is not a name-it-and-claim-it belief system or a religion that says, "If you believe hard enough, it will all work out." This is about raising your eyes above your circumstances. We often become so entangled in what's happening and not happening or what we should and shouldn't do, we forget to stop. We forget to refocus on God's promise in the midst of our thoughts, fears, and the lack of fulfillment of God's promise to us. It does not matter one iota if it is impossible to the God who does not know what impossible is.

Read Psalm 121 in the the translation provided. Let it wash over you. Sarah never got to read these words, but we do.

> I look up at the vast size of the mountains—from where will my help come in times of trouble? The Eternal Creator of heaven and earth and these mountains will send the help I need. He holds you firmly in place; He will not let you fall. He who keeps you will never take His eyes off you and never drift off to sleep. What a relief! The One who watches over Israel never leaves for rest or sleep. The

Eternal keeps you safe, so close to Him that His shadow is a cooling shade to you. Neither bright light of sun nor dim light of moon will harm you. The Eternal will keep you safe from all of life's evils, From your first breath to the last breath you breathe, from this day and forever. (The Voice)

What obstacle do you need to look over in order to look up to the God who holds the promise that has been given to you?

_____

_____

_____

_____

What are some practical steps you can take as you endure the long wait? For example, I've had to learn to turn my thoughts from the impossible to "all things are possible with God". Fill in the blanks below with what you feel you are coming against and what God's truth has stated.

Lord,

I feel_____, but I know that is not true because Your Word says_____. Father, thank You that You see the end from the beginning and make a way when there seems to be no way. I love You dearly and need You desperately. Make a way today, God. Help me to see that You are enough for today.

WEEK 2

HANNAH
Waiting in the Midst of Insult

Does this sound familiar to you? You're hurting, struggling, and longing for something that you know only God can provide. Then someone comes along and takes you out at the knees with poorly placed advice or an unhelpful anecdote. They don't want to uplift and edify. They want to strike a blow and bruise your soul. You've met this person. Maybe you are this person.

Hannah was the recipient of nonstop verbal blows from another woman. It's hard to read her story and not be moved to tears over her anguish. She felt utterly alone in her pain, and the one person who could have easily come alongside her to be her greatest encourager never let up, but instead, she chose to be her greatest opposition. This week, notice the humility of Hannah's plight before God and her gracious response to the insults that were thrown on her. Pay attention to the types of words found in this passage and the ways that they can influence us.

DAY 1

FIGHTING WORDS

Ask the Holy Spirit to give you ears to hear, eyes to see, and a heart that is open to His Word. Read 1 Samuel 1:1–28 and 2:1–11 in your own Bible.

Let me give you a personal example of how waiting has played a role in my life. I'm thirty-three, I'm single, and I have no children yet. Now, I don't want to be single and childless forever, but God has determined that it is best for this season of my life. Therefore, I am living my life to the fullest and approaching these days as a gift and not as a waste of time.

Of course, like many in my situation, I long to be a wife and mother. I long for relationship and intimacy. On my best days, I don't allow it to consume my thoughts, but it's never far from them. Does that make sense? Do you do this too when you deeply desire something?

As a pediatric nurse, I live and breathe taking care of children. I may not have my own baby in my arms yet, but I have a mother's heart, and I constantly need to place myself in a mother's shoes. Parents of my patients often ask me, "Do you have kids?" Although I know they are simply trying to make conversation, I feel a twinge of pain every time.

My mind starts to spiral as I think, *Do they think that I would treat their child differently if I did? Do they think I'm being too rough with their child? Do they think that I'm doing a really good job with their child?*

I feel a pang because they don't know my story. They don't know my desires and longings. Barrenness, miscarriages, and infertility are not my current situations, but it might be yours.

Recently, I changed roles at my hospital. I was placed on a team where I was working with women who were old enough to be my mom. Over the course of a few months, my coworkers started to give me advice: "Oh, it's different when you have kids." In one situation, I tried to calm nervous family members multiple times. Then I had to step away to help another family. One of my coworkers told my patient's family, "I'll go check on your daughter. I'm a mom, too."

Those comments made me feel as if I was less than my coworkers were and like I couldn't have a mother's level of empathy or care. Just because I couldn't identify did not mean that I could not empathize. The kicker came when a coworker told me right in front of a family, "You didn't think of that because you're not a mom!"

Knives—all those comments felt like hot, searing blades that were intentionally shoved right into my heart. In fact, I would rather be physically hurt than to hear those words over and over.

Here's the thing. When parents said it, I didn't like it, but I knew they weren't intentionally trying to hurt me. When a coworker, fellow nurse, and friend said it, it was horribly insulting and hurtful because that person knew how much I would love to have a family of my own. Some of them were choosing to put a hot, searing knife into a tender area. Can you imagine how I would feel if that individual had brought me cool, refreshing water with their words instead of wounds.

Multiply it one-thousand times, and that's where we find Hannah. In 1 Samuel, Hannah was introduced as Elkanah's wife. Much like Sarah, her womb had been closed by God, and she had borne no children. During this time in history, being married and having children—especially sons—were a woman's primary markers for success and security in society.

Elkanah had another wife, Peninnah, who had multiple children. For Hannah, feelings of disappointment, shame, and worthlessness were present. She had to deal with not bearing a child. Her situation was made worse by the terrorizing words launched at her from the other wife.

Again, we bristle at the thought of a man having more than one wife, but it's important to take into consideration the cultural context of this story. Don't get hung up on those things for now. Instead, look for the overarching theme. Then go back and dig deeper into what their lives looked like on a daily basis.

*When there is pain involved, it's hard for us to
understand that God is doing it FOR us.*

First Samuel 1:6–7 says,

> And because the LORD had closed her womb, her rival kept provoking her in order to irritate her. This went on year after year. Whenever Hannah went to the house of the Lord, her rival provoked her till she wept and would not eat.

In the verse above, highlight any terms that deal with time. Circle the actions of Peninnah. Underline Hannah's responses.

Is there someone in your life who is provoking you or intentionally inflicting hurtful wounds? If there is not someone doing this now, can you think of a past situation where you were the target?

_____

_____

_____

_____

What is your response? Don't write what you think you should do, ought to do, or want to do. Answer honestly.

> Jesus,
>
> Take hold of my heart as I pour out the things that have been said and done to me and that have wounded me deeply. Give me courage to walk with you through this situation and keep my eyes focused on you.

New Living Translation (NLT)

There was a man named Elkanah who lived in Ramah in the region of Zuph in the hill country of Ephraim. He was the son of Jeroham, son of Elihu, son of Tohu, son of Zuph, of Ephraim. Elkanah had two wives, Hannah and Peninnah. Peninnah had children, but Hannah did not. Each year Elkanah would travel to Shiloh to worship and sacrifice to the Lord of Heaven's Armies at the Tabernacle. The priests of the Lord at that time were the two sons of Eli—Hophni and Phinehas. On the days Elkanah presented his sacrifice, he would give portions of the meat to Peninnah and each of her children. And though he loved Hannah, he would give her only one choice portion because the Lord had given her no children. So Peninnah would taunt Hannah and make fun of her because the Lord had kept her from having children. Year after year it was the same—Peninnah would taunt Hannah as they went to the Tabernacle. Each time, Hannah would be reduced to tears and would not even eat. "Why are you crying, Hannah?" Elkanah would ask. "Why aren't you eating? Why be downhearted just because you have no children? You have me—isn't that better than having ten sons?"

Hannah's Prayer for a Son

Once after a sacrificial meal at Shiloh, Hannah got up and went to pray. Eli the priest was sitting at his customary place beside the entrance of the Tabernacle. Hannah was in deep anguish, crying bitterly as she prayed to the Lord. And she made this vow: "O Lord of Heaven's Armies, if you will look upon my sorrow and answer my prayer and give me a son, then I will give him back to you. He will be yours for his entire lifetime, and as a sign that he has been dedicated to the Lord, his hair will never be cut." As she was praying to the Lord, Eli watched her. Seeing her lips moving but hearing no sound, he thought she had been drinking. "Must you come here drunk?" he demanded. "Throw away your wine!" "Oh no, sir!" she replied. "I haven't been drinking wine or anything stronger. But I am very discouraged, and I was pouring out my heart to the Lord. Don't think I am a wicked woman! For I have been praying out of great anguish and sorrow." "In that case," Eli said, "go in peace! May the God of Israel grant the request you have asked of him." "Oh, thank you, sir!" she exclaimed. Then she went back and began to eat again, and she was no longer sad.

Samuel's Birth and Dedication

The entire family got up early the next morning and went to worship the Lord once more. Then they returned home to Ramah. When Elkanah slept with Hannah, the Lord remembered her plea, and in due time she gave birth to a son. She named him Samuel, for she said, "I asked the Lord for him." The next year Elkanah and his family went on their annual trip to offer a sacrifice to the

Lord and to keep his vow. But Hannah did not go. She told her husband, "Wait until the boy is weaned. Then I will take him to the Tabernacle and leave him there with the Lord permanently." "Whatever you think is best," Elkanah agreed. "Stay here for now, and may the Lord help you keep your promise." So she stayed home and nursed the boy until he was weaned. When the child was weaned, Hannah took him to the Tabernacle in Shiloh. They brought along a three-year-old bull for the sacrifice and a basket of flour and some wine. After sacrificing the bull, they brought the boy to Eli. "Sir, do you remember me?" Hannah asked. "I am the very woman who stood here several years ago praying to the Lord. I asked the Lord to give me this boy, and he has granted my request. Now I am giving him to the Lord, and he will belong to the Lord his whole life." And they worshiped the Lord there.

Hannah's Prayer of Praise

Then Hannah prayed: "My heart rejoices in the Lord! The Lord has made me strong. Now I have an answer for my enemies; I rejoice because you rescued me. No one is holy like the Lord! There is no one besides you; there is no Rock like our God. Stop acting so proud and haughty! Don't speak with such arrogance! For the Lord is a God who knows what you have done; he will judge your actions. The bow of the mighty is now broken, and those who stumbled are now strong. Those who were well fed are now starving, and those who were starving are now full. The childless woman now has seven children, and the woman with many children wastes away. The Lord gives both death and life; he brings some down to the grave but raises others up. The Lord makes some poor and others rich; he brings some down and lifts others up. He lifts the poor from the dust and the needy from the garbage dump. He sets them among princes, placing them in seats of honor. For all the earth is the Lord's, and he has set the world in order. He will protect his faithful ones, but the wicked will disappear in darkness. No one will succeed by strength alone. Those who fight against the Lord will be shattered. He thunders against them from heaven; the Lord judges throughout the earth. He gives power to his king; he increases the strength of his anointed one." (1 Samuel 1–2:11)

DAY 2

HONEST WORDS

Ask the Holy Spirit to give you ears to hear, eyes to see, and a heart that is open to His Word. Read 1 Samuel 1:1–28 and 2:1–11 in the text provided.

In her absolute brokenness, Hannah continued to pray and plead for a son. She made a vow to dedicate the child wholly to God.

How often did this happen? (verses 6–7)

_____

_____

_____

_____

In verses 7, 8, and 10, the word used for *weep* is the Hebrew word *bakah*. It means, "To weep, bewail, cry, shed tears," and it is used with, "Grief or humiliation."[10] I think it's safe to say that we can find Hannah in that place. We can find ourselves there too. It is an utterly shattered place filled with sobs and total confusion as to why God, our Father, is delaying a response to us.

Focus on 1 Samuel 1:1–18.

Because she was so focused in prayer, Hannah was moving her lips but not speaking. The priest assumed that she was _____.

Drunk! And it was being done in their holy place, no less. This added insult to injury for Hannah. She was scorned by her husband's other wife, and now in the one place where she felt most honest and safe, she was accused of being drunk by the priest.

When was the last time you felt like someone kicked you when you were already down? What was your response?

_____

_____

_____

_____

Hannah's response was one of the most beautiful responses in all scripture because in that shattered, tired, Valley of Baca, there was a pure heart, a humble spirit, and a soul filled with faith. She chose to use honest words to explain herself and not self-deprecating, defensive, cowering, aggressive, or vague words.

> "Not so, my LORD," Hannah replied, "I am a woman who is deeply troubled. I have not been drinking wine or beer; I was pouring out my soul to the LORD. Do not take your servant for a wicked (worthless) woman; I have been praying here out of my great anguish and grief."
>
> (1 Samuel 1:15–16)

We do not need to be afraid of what the Lord will do when we weep.

May we be quick to enter these same spaces with purity and humility of heart. Our dreams, disappointments, and desires are so safe there. He guards them and bottles our tears. We can know that He defends us tirelessly. While we may have people in our lives whom we feel that we can be honest with, we always run the risk of the relationship breaking up. God is big enough to take our honest fears, thoughts, and beliefs and not be so hurt that He walks away. Instead, He stays with you there and walks with you through it.

Hopefully, you noticed the Hebrew word *bakah* and then the mention of the Valley of Baca. One is the root word of the other. Both mean *weeping*. Psalm 84:6–7 tells us that, "As they go through the Valley of Baca, he provides a spring for them. The rain even covers it with pools of water. They are sustained as they go along" (The Voice).

A more well-known version (the New International Version) says,

They go from _____ to _____."

Year after year, Hannah went from strength to strength, and she was sustained by her Almighty God. The waiting is hard, but God promised to give us strength.

Write out a prayer to God that reminds you of your strength-to-strength moments and gratefulness for God constantly sustaining you during your wait. Use honest words to tell God about your Valley of Baca and ask Him to lead you to His Word. Read the honest words that He speaks over you and take them personally. He is a personal and intimate God.

_____

_____

_____

_____

New American Standard Bible (NASB)

Now there was a certain man from Ramathaim-zophim from the hill country of Ephraim, and his name was Elkanah the son of Jeroham, the son of Elihu, the son of Tohu, the son of Zuph, an Ephraimite. He had two wives: the name of one was Hannah and the name of the other Peninnah; and Peninnah had children, but Hannah had no children. Now this man would go up from his city yearly to worship and to sacrifice to the Lord of hosts in Shiloh. And the two sons of Eli, Hophni and Phinehas, were priests to the Lord there. When the day came that Elkanah sacrificed, he would give portions to Peninnah his wife and to all her sons and her daughters; but to Hannah he would give a double portion, for he loved Hannah, but the Lord had closed her womb. Her rival, however, would provoke her bitterly to irritate her, because the Lord had closed her womb. It happened year after year, as often as she went up to the house of the Lord, she would provoke her; so she wept and would not eat. Then Elkanah her husband said to her, "Hannah, why do you weep and why do you not eat and why is your heart sad? Am I not better to you than ten sons?" Then Hannah rose after eating and drinking in Shiloh. Now Eli the priest was sitting on the seat by the doorpost of the temple of the Lord. She, greatly distressed, prayed to the Lord and wept bitterly. She made a vow and said, "O Lord of hosts, if You will indeed look on the affliction of Your maidservant and remember me, and not forget Your maidservant, but will give Your maidservant a son, then I will give him to the Lord all the days of his life, and a razor shall never come on his head." Now it came about, as she continued praying before the Lord, that Eli was watching her mouth. As for Hannah, she was speaking in her heart, only her lips were moving, but her voice was not heard. So Eli thought she was drunk. Then Eli said to her, "How long will you make yourself drunk? Put away your wine from you." But Hannah replied, "No, my lord, I am a woman oppressed in spirit; I have drunk neither wine nor strong drink, but I have poured out my soul before the Lord. Do not consider your maidservant as a worthless woman, for I have spoken until now out of my great concern and provocation." Then Eli answered and said, "Go in peace; and may the God of Israel grant your petition that you have asked of Him." She said, "Let your maidservant find favor in your sight." So the woman went her way and ate, and her face was no longer sad.

Samuel Is Born to Hannah

Then they arose early in the morning and worshiped before the Lord, and returned again to their house in Ramah. And Elkanah had relations with Hannah his wife, and the Lord remembered her. It came about in due time, after Hannah had conceived, that she gave birth to a son; and she named him Samuel, saying, "Because I have asked him of the Lord." Then the man Elkanah went up with all his household to offer to the Lord the yearly sacrifice and pay his vow. But Hannah did not go up, for she said to her husband, "I will not go up until the child is weaned; then I will bring him, that he may appear before the Lord and stay there forever." Elkanah her husband said to her, "Do what seems best to you. Remain until you have weaned him; only may the Lord confirm His word." So the woman remained and nursed her son until she weaned him. Now when she had weaned him, she took him up with her, with a three-year-old bull and one ephah of flour and a jug of wine, and brought him to the house of the Lord in Shiloh, although the child was young. Then they slaughtered the bull, and brought the boy to Eli. She said, "Oh, my lord! As your soul lives, my lord, I am the woman who stood here beside you, praying to the Lord. For this boy I prayed, and the Lord has given me my petition which I asked of Him. So I have also dedicated him to the Lord; as long as he lives he is dedicated to the Lord." And he worshiped the Lord there.

Hannah's Song of Thanksgiving

Then Hannah prayed and said, "My heart exults in the Lord; My horn is exalted in the Lord, My mouth speaks boldly against my enemies, Because I rejoice in Your salvation. "There is no one holy like the Lord, Indeed, there is no one besides You, Nor is there any rock like our God. Boast no more so very proudly, Do not let arrogance come out of your mouth; For the Lord is a God of knowledge, And with Him actions are weighed. "The bows of the mighty are shattered, But the feeble gird on strength. Those who were full hire themselves out for bread, But those who were hungry cease to hunger. Even the barren gives birth to seven, But she who has many children languishes. The Lord kills and makes alive; He brings down to Sheol and raises up. The Lord makes poor and rich; He brings low, He also exalts. He raises the poor from the dust, He lifts the needy from the ash heap to make them sit with nobles, And inherit a seat of honor; For the pillars of the earth are the Lord's, And He set the world on them. He keeps the feet of His godly ones, But the wicked ones are silenced in darkness; For not by might shall a man prevail. Those who contend with the Lord will be shattered; Against them He will thunder in the heavens, The Lord will judge the ends of the earth; And He will give strength to His king, And will exalt the horn of His anointed." Then Elkanah went to his home at Ramah. But the boy ministered to the Lord before Eli the priest. (1 Samuel 1–2:11)

DAY 3

INTENTIONAL WORDS

Ask the Holy Spirit to give you ears to hear, eyes to see, and a heart that is open to His Word. Read 1 Samuel 1:1–28 and 2:1–11 in the text provided.

Like all of us, Hannah just wanted to be heard and remembered by her God. When she revealed to Eli how troubled she was and poured out her soul to the Lord, how did He respond to her? (1 Samuel 1:15)

_____

_____

_____

_____

Here is a great mini-lesson that is too good to pass up. When we as believers see others who are struggling, we should not only come alongside and meet their needs but also show compassion and *ask the Lord* to grant their requests. Often, the first thing we say is, "Oh, I'll pray about that for you," and by the time the conversation ends, our thoughts have as well, along with our intentions to pray on their behalves.

It's OK to be so moved with compassion that you stop the conversation or end the pouring out of their souls so that you can pray on their behalves. One of our greatest honors is to bring our brothers and sisters before the throne and intercede for them. You will never go wrong with prayer. Meet tangible needs, of course, but pray without ceasing.

Ok, now let's get back to Hannah. She was a woman of prayer. She was relentless in it. How many times is a form of the word pray used in 1 Samuel 1:9–16?

_____

_____

_____

_____

What are you relentless in? Is it your own thoughts? Do you talk to your closest friends about it over and over?

_____

_____

_____

_____

The goal here isn't to make you feel bad, but it's to recognize that Hannah serves as a standard for us. The text only records her talking to God about her pain.

Now I am sure that she and Elkanah had plenty of conversations about the subject, but she knew that Elkanah could not get to the heart of the issue. She did not expect him to have the answers. He had proved his love for his wife repeatedly as he tried to comfort her, offer her more than he did Peninnah, and gave her whatever he was able to give.

He could not control whether or not she could conceive. Neither of them could, and Hannah knew it. However, she knew her Father could, so she had no problem asking Him.

Eventually and "in the course of time," Hannah conceived and dedicated her son, Samuel, to the Lord (1 Samuel 1:20). After she took him to the house of the LORD, we do not know what was going on in Hannah's heart as she handed over her dear son—the desire she had had for so long—and left him in the arms of another.

However, she had made a vow to God and honored it. She believed that God was in control, and she trusted God with her much-pled-for son. While we don't know what she felt in that moment, we are able to read her response. She worshipped and prayed. Did you notice that?

Before, during, and after, prayer was her default language.

Focus on 1 Samuel 2:1–10.

> Do not keep talking so _____ or let your mouth speak such _____,
> the LORD is a God who knows, and by him deeds are weighed. (1 Samuel 2:3)

Hannah is not being snarky or sassy. She is calling attention to what God has done for her. She is being intentional.

There will be a day when we will get to celebrate in victory over our enemies, who have accused us of things. We will get to say, "The LORD is a God who knows, and by Him deeds are weighed" (1 Samuel 2:3). Our God knows and secures us. Only He has the final say over our identities.

Using Hannah's response as a model, what can you say back to the enemy who is relentlessly accusing you?

_____

_____

_____

_____

Jesus,

In these moments when someone has spoken of or against me, remind me that You are the ultimate authority. Help me to always praise You first and in advance of what You are about to do. When days seem especially hard and dark, help me recall Your words in Revelation 19 and 20, where You bring an end to the torture that is happening on Earth to Your children. I wait for Your return, Jesus.

New King James Version (NKJV)

Now there was a certain man of Ramathaim Zophim, of the mountains of Ephraim, and his name was Elkanah the son of Jeroham, the son of Elihu, the son of Tohu, the son of Zuph, an Ephraimite. And he had two wives: the name of one was Hannah, and the name of the other Peninnah. Peninnah had children, but Hannah had no children. This man went up from his city yearly to worship and sacrifice to the Lord of hosts in Shiloh. Also the two sons of Eli, Hophni and Phinehas, the priests of the Lord, were there. And whenever the time came for Elkanah to make an offering, he would give portions to Peninnah his wife and to all her sons and daughters. But to Hannah he would give a double portion, for he loved Hannah, although the Lord had closed her womb. And her rival also provoked her severely, to make her miserable, because the Lord had closed her womb. So it was, year by year, when she went up to the house of the Lord, that she provoked her; therefore she wept and did not eat.

Hannah's Vow

Then Elkanah her husband said to her, "Hannah, why do you weep? Why do you not eat? And why is your heart grieved? Am I not better to you than ten sons?" So Hannah arose after they had finished eating and drinking in Shiloh. Now Eli the priest was sitting on the seat by the doorpost of the tabernacle of the Lord. And she was in bitterness of soul, and prayed to the Lord and wept in anguish. Then she made a vow and said, "O Lord of hosts, if You will indeed look on the affliction of Your maidservant and remember me, and not forget Your maidservant, but will give Your maidservant a male child, then I will give him to the Lord all the days of his life, and no razor shall come upon his head." And it happened, as she continued praying before the Lord, that Eli watched her mouth. Now Hannah spoke in her heart; only her lips moved, but her voice was not heard. Therefore Eli thought she was drunk. So Eli said to her, "How long will you be drunk? Put your wine away from you!" But Hannah answered and said, "No, my lord, I am a woman of sorrowful spirit. I have drunk neither wine nor intoxicating drink, but have poured out my soul before the Lord. Do not consider your maidservant a wicked woman, for out of the abundance of my complaint and grief I have spoken until now." Then Eli answered and said, "Go in peace, and the God of Israel grant your petition which you have asked of Him." And she said, "Let your maidservant find favor in your sight." So the woman went her way and ate, and her face was no longer sad.

Samuel Is Born and Dedicated

Then they rose early in the morning and worshiped before the Lord, and returned and came to their house at Ramah. And Elkanah knew Hannah his wife, and the Lord remembered her. So it came to pass in the process of time that Hannah conceived and bore a son, and called his name Samuel, saying, "Because I have asked for him from the Lord." Now the man Elkanah and all his house went up to offer to the Lord the yearly sacrifice and his vow. But Hannah did not go up, for she said to her husband, "Not until the child is weaned; then I will take him, that he may appear before the Lord and remain there forever." So Elkanah her husband said to her, "Do what seems best to you; wait until you have weaned him. Only let the Lord establish His word." Then the woman stayed and nursed her son until she had weaned him. Now when she had weaned him, she took him up with her, with three bulls, one ephah of flour, and a skin of wine, and brought him to the house of the Lord in Shiloh. And the child was young. Then they slaughtered a bull, and brought the child to Eli. And she said, "O my lord! As your soul lives, my lord, I am the woman who stood by you here, praying to the Lord. For this child I prayed, and the Lord has granted me my petition which I asked of Him. Therefore I also have lent him to the Lord; as long as he lives he shall be lent to the Lord." So they worshiped the Lord there.

Hannah's Prayer

And Hannah prayed and said: "My heart rejoices in the Lord; My horn is exalted in the Lord. I smile at my enemies, Because I rejoice in Your salvation. No one is holy like the Lord, For there is none besides You, Nor is there any rock like our God. Talk no more so very proudly; Let no arrogance come from your mouth, For the Lord is the God of knowledge; And by Him actions are weighed. The bows of the mighty men are broken, And those who stumbled are girded with strength. Those who were full have hired themselves out for bread, And the hungry have ceased to hunger. Even the barren has borne seven, And she who has many children has become feeble. The Lord kills and makes alive; He brings down to the grave and brings up. The Lord makes poor and makes rich; He brings low and lifts up. He raises the poor from the dust And lifts the beggar from the ash heap, To set them among princes And make them inherit the throne of glory. For the pillars of the earth are the Lord's, And He has set the world upon them. He will guard the feet of His saints, But the wicked shall be silent in darkness. For by strength no man shall prevail. The adversaries of the Lord shall be broken in pieces; From heaven He will thunder against them. The Lord will judge the ends of the earth. He will give strength to His king, And exalt the horn of His anointed." Then Elkanah went to his house at Ramah. But the child ministered to the Lord before Eli the priest. (1 Samuel 1–2:11)

DAY 4

TRUSTING WORDS

Ask the Holy Spirit to give you ears to hear, eyes to see, and a heart that is open to His Word. Read 1 Samuel 1:1–28 and 2:1–11 in the text that is provided.

Hannah gave us a beautiful example of how to wait well. Do you think that she wanted to be vindicated and considered equal with Peninnah? Of course she did! However, there is no record of Hannah lashing out toward her or her children.

Instead of returning insult for insult or trying to take matters into her own hands, Hannah did the only thing that she knew could make a difference: She went directly to the source of life. She took her frustration, hurt, and rejection to the Lord in prayer. She told God everything and then humbly asked that He would step in and change her circumstances.

How prone are you to do the same thing? Do you swallow your insults and take them to God, or do you need to say hurtful things?

_____

_____

_____

_____

Be honest with yourself. Have you learned how to be honest and clear when you disapprove of someone or something without slandering or intentionally tearing that person down?

_____

_____

_____

_____

Can we talk about something that is *really* hard? What does the Bible explicitly state in 1 Samuel 1:5?

_____

_____

_____

_____

God shut her womb. Why did He do that? He gave her the desire in the first place, right? So why would God withhold from Hannah the thing that she desired most?

_____

_____

_____

_____

Do not be deceived, my friend.

> *For the LORD God is a sun and shield; The LORD gives*
> *grace and glory; <u>No good thing does He withhold</u> from those*
> *who walk uprightly. (Psalm 84:11, emphasis is mine)*

It can be hard to accept that sometimes God uses the absolute hardest of circumstances to prepare us for the place He wants us to go. If Hannah's womb had not been closed, would she have experienced a deeply intimate walk with her Creator year after year? Would she have seen her need for rescue? Her pain led to her greatest pride. She would give birth to one of the greatest prophets the world has ever known: Samuel.

Read 1 Samuel 16:1–13. What did Samuel do?

_____

_____

_____

_____

Read 2 Samuel 7:16. What did God tell David?

_____

_____

_____

_____

Read Matthew 1:1, Romans 1:3, and 2 Timothy 2:8. Whose line does this assure us that Jesus descended from?

_____

_____

_____

_____

In her pain, she was honest and intentional, she trusted God, and she used her words to express it. Her prayer was answered by the birth of Samuel, which later led to David being crowned king and the Davidic covenant. This covenant paved the way for us to have a greater understanding of the new covenant in Jesus Christ.

How have you learned that things done *by* God are actually done *for* you and not *to* you?

_____

_____

_____

_____

God did not delight in Hannah's agony. He is always at work, and He knows every detail from the beginning to the end. Hannah recognized this and raised her eyes above her circumstance. She raised her gaze to the One who could change it. She did not view herself as a victim, but instead, she prayed and asked God to intervene on her behalf.

What good Father does not hear the cries of His children? She did not use her childlessness as an excuse to exclude herself from God's greater story. Moments of pain turned into moments of power as she entrusted her own life and the lives of her husband and son into the hands of her Heavenly Father.

Either we know in our bones that God is in control of every area of our lives, or we don't. He's sovereign and supreme over our circumstances, our struggling relationships, the course that we just can't seem to understand, our family member who is breaking the other family member's hearts, our continual provocation by someone who is being used by the enemy, and even our closed wombs.

God determines what is good, and we do not. By all means, we can ask God and trust Him to intervene in it, but we do not have the right to tell Him what we think is the best plan.

> Father,
>
> Just as Your people faced horrific suffering and destruction, my body and mind feel like they are suffering and on the verge of destruction. Your word says,
>
> I remember my affliction and my wandering, the bitterness and the gall. I well remember them, and my soul is downcast within me. Yet this I call to mind and therefore I have hope: Because of the Lord's great love we are not consumed, for his compassions never fail. They are new every morning; great is your faithfulness. I say to myself, "The Lord is my portion; therefore I will wait for him." The Lord is good to those whose hope is in him, to the one who seeks him; it is good to wait quietly for the salvation of the Lord.
>
> (Lamentations 3:19–26)
>
> I trust You, Father, and I use my words to confess that truth.

The Message (MSG)

There once was a man who lived in Ramathaim. He was descended from the old Zuph family in the Ephraim hills. His name was Elkanah. (He was connected with the Zuphs from Ephraim through his father Jeroham, his grandfather Elihu, and his great-grandfather Tohu.) He had two wives. The first was Hannah; the second was Peninnah. Peninnah had children; Hannah did not. Every year this man went from his hometown up to Shiloh to worship and offer a sacrifice to God-of-the-Angel-Armies. Eli and his two sons, Hophni and Phinehas, served as the priests of God there. When Elkanah sacrificed, he passed helpings from the sacrificial meal around to his wife Peninnah and all her children, but he always gave an especially generous helping to Hannah because he loved her so much, and because God had not given her children. But her rival wife taunted her cruelly, rubbing it in and never letting her forget that God had not given her children. This went on year after year. Every time she went to the sanctuary of God she could expect to be taunted. Hannah was reduced to tears and had no appetite. Her husband Elkanah said, "Oh, Hannah, why are you crying? Why aren't you eating? And why are you so upset? Am I not of more worth to you than ten sons?" So Hannah ate. Then she pulled herself together, slipped away quietly, and entered the sanctuary. The priest Eli was on duty at the entrance to God's Temple in the customary seat. Crushed in soul, Hannah prayed to God and cried and cried—inconsolably. Then she made a vow: Oh, God-of-the- Angel-Armies, If you'll take a good, hard look at my pain, If you'll quit neglecting me and go into action for me By giving me a son, I'll give him completely, unreservedly to you. I'll set him apart for a life of holy discipline. It so happened that as she continued in prayer before God, Eli was watching her closely. Hannah was praying in her heart, silently. Her lips moved, but no sound was heard. Eli jumped to the conclusion that she was drunk. He approached her and said, "You're drunk! How long do you plan to keep this up? Sober up, woman!" Hannah said, "Oh no, sir—please! I'm a woman hard used. I haven't been drinking. Not a drop of wine or beer. The only thing I've been pouring out is my heart, pouring it out to God. Don't for a minute think I'm a bad woman. It's because I'm so desperately unhappy and in such pain that I've stayed here so long." Eli answered her, "Go in peace. And may the God of Israel give you what you have asked of him." "Think well of me—and pray for me!" she said, and went her way. Then she ate heartily, her face radiant. Up before dawn, they worshiped God and returned home to Ramah. Elkanah slept with Hannah his wife, and God began making the necessary arrangements in response to what she had asked.

Dedicating the Child to God

Before the year was out, Hannah had conceived and given birth to a son. She named him Samuel, explaining, "I asked God for him." When Elkanah next took his family on their annual trip to

Shiloh to worship God, offering sacrifices and keeping his vow, Hannah didn't go. She told her husband, "After the child is weaned, I'll bring him myself and present him before God—and that's where he'll stay, for good." Elkanah said to his wife, "Do what you think is best. Stay home until you have weaned him. Yes! Let God complete what he has begun!" So she did. She stayed home and nursed her son until she had weaned him. Then she took him up to Shiloh, bringing also the makings of a generous sacrificial meal—a prize bull, flour, and wine. The child was so young to be sent off! They first butchered the bull, then brought the child to Eli. Hannah said, "Excuse me, sir. Would you believe that I'm the very woman who was standing before you at this very spot, praying to God? I prayed for this child, and God gave me what I asked for. And now I have dedicated him to God. He's dedicated to God for life." Then and there, they worshiped God.

Hannah prayed:

I'm bursting with God-news! I'm walking on air. I'm laughing at my rivals. I'm dancing my salvation. Nothing and no one is holy like God, no rock mountain like our God. Don't dare talk pretentiously—not a word of boasting, ever! For God knows what's going on. He takes the measure of everything that happens. The weapons of the strong are smashed to pieces, while the weak are infused with fresh strength. The well-fed are out begging in the streets for crusts, while the hungry are getting second helpings. The barren woman has a houseful of children, while the mother of many is bereft. God brings death and God brings life, brings down to the grave and raises up. God brings poverty and God brings wealth; he lowers, he also lifts up. He puts poor people on their feet again; he rekindles burned-out lives with fresh hope, Restoring dignity and respect to their lives—a place in the sun! For the very structures of earth are God's; he has laid out his operations on a firm foundation. He protectively cares for his faithful friends, step by step, but leaves the wicked to stumble in the dark. No one makes it in this life by sheer muscle! God's enemies will be blasted out of the sky, crashed in a heap and burned. God will set things right all over the earth, he'll give strength to his king, he'll set his anointed on top of the world!

> Elkanah went home to Ramah. The boy stayed and served God in the company of Eli the priest.

(1 Samuel 1–2:11)

DAY 5

WORSHIPFUL WORDS

Ask the Holy Spirit to give you ears to hear, eyes to see, and a heart that is open to His Word. Read 1 Samuel 1:1–28 and 2:1–11 in the text that is provided.

As fiercely as Hannah prayed, she worshipped God mightily and praised Him for all He had done. When she did not have an actual promise in hand, she had faith that God would hear her and trusted that He cared about her deepest desires. She allowed hope to arise and God to work in His time. Then she followed His action with praise.

Hannah taught us the value of an unrelenting belief in a God who heard the cries of His child. He knows our entire situations, and He has designed a larger story, which will ultimately be for our good. Believing this to the core allows us to rest and have peace in the Almighty's hands.

Today will look different from the previous days. We are going to read words that are worship to God. Read them three times. The first time, read them silently. The second time, speak them out. The third time, pray them. If you are having a hard time using your words to worship God, ask Him to change your heart and replace destructive words toward yourself or others with worship.

Psalm 34 was written long after Hannah's time, but the beautiful thing about the scripture is that it is harmonious in its message. Below, read that things that the Lord longs to do for you! Circle, highlight, mark up, and make notes. He wants to speak to you!

Lord!

I will extol the Lord at all times; his praise will always be on my lips. I will glory in the Lord; let the afflicted hear and rejoice. Glorify the Lord with me; let us exalt his name together. I sought the Lord, and he answered me; he delivered me from all my fears. Those who look to him are radiant; their faces are never covered with shame. This poor man called, and the Lord heard him; he saved him out of all his troubles. The angel of the Lord encamps around those who fear him, and he delivers them. Taste and see that the Lord is good; blessed is the one who takes refuge in him. Fear the Lord, you his holy people, for those who fear him lack nothing. The lions may grow weak and hungry, but those who seek the Lord lack no good thing. Come, my children, listen to me; I will teach you the fear of the Lord. Whoever of you loves life and desires to see many good days, keep your tongue from evil and your lips from telling lies. Turn from evil and do good; seek peace and pursue it. The eyes of the Lord are on the righteous, and his ears are attentive to their cry; but the face of the Lord is against those who do evil, to blot out their name from the earth. The righteous cry out, and the Lord hears them; he delivers them from all their troubles. The Lord is close to the brokenhearted and saves those who are crushed in spirit. The righteous person may have many troubles, but the Lord delivers him from them all; he protects all his bones, not one of them will be broken. Evil will slay the wicked; the foes of the righteous will be condemned. The Lord will rescue his servants; no one who takes refuge in him will be condemned. (NLT)

This week, we have learned that the words we choose to use matter. Being a wordy woman myself, I have to be so careful. I make a conscious effort to let only some things come out of my mouth. My tone matters and motives matter. The things that come out of my mouth will either build walls or tear them down.

In my waiting, I have resolved not to be a victim, but instead, I will trust that God is sovereign and use my words to praise Him for the authority that He holds over my life. Psalm 34 reminds me not to dwell on what I don't yet have but instead, to worship my King for all He has done. He has done *great* things!

WEEK 3

MARY, THE MOTHER OF JESUS
Waiting in the Midst of the Unknown

If you ask anyone what the hardest part about waiting is, one of the most frequent answers is, "Fear of the unknown." Nothing in this life comes with absolute certainty, whether it's the business deal being pulled off, the meeting with someone special, or the medical scans coming back negative. When it comes to the future, we just don't have guarantees.

Let's take a closer look at one of the most revered woman in history, Mary, the mother of Jesus. Sure, we look back on her faith with amazement now, but her life was anything but a pretty picture. She was a pregnant virgin engaged to a man who had every right to ditch her. She would potentially bring shame on her family. Let's just all be glad that social media wasn't a thing yet. Most of us are very uncomfortable with the unknown, but we can learn a lesson or two from Mary, who showed that she trusted God and His timing.

DAY 1

FAITH RESPONDS

Ask the Holy Spirit to give you ears to hear, eyes to see, and a heart that is open to His Word. Read Luke 1:1–56 in your own Bible.

What is your current unknown?

_____

_____

_____

_____

How do you feel about that unknown? Anxious? Confident?

_____

_____

_____

_____

Focus on verses 26–55. After the four hundred years of the intertestamental period, which was its own massive story about waiting and trusting God for the fulfillment of His promise in the coming Messiah, the gospels introduce us to a young teenager named Mary. She was divinely informed that she would conceive a baby by the Holy Spirit, thus fulfilling the centuries' old prophecy in Isaiah 7:14.[11]

Unlike many that had gone before her, Mary had no problem believing the promise the Lord had given her and immediately accepted it as truth. Nevertheless, she faced an incomparable season of waiting. Six months earlier, Mary's relative Elizabeth had been about to conceive as well, but her husband, Zechariah, had had a hard time with the news.

How did Mary's response differ from Zechariah's response?

_____

_____

_____

_____

To be honest, this question confused me for years. How were their responses different when both of them asked a similar question: "How?" Compare Luke 1:11–20 to Luke 1:26–38. Write the similarities and differences below.

_____

_____

_____

_____

The answer is found in verse 20, where it says, "But you did not believe my words," and in verse 38, where it says, "May it be to me as you have said." Faith is the difference. Zechariah showed a lack of faith when he asked his question.

I can understand him being caught up in the moment and forgetting that many have had children when they were well past their primes, including Abraham, the founding father of the faith and someone whom a priest would have been well acquainted. But when God sought faith, Zechariah expressed doubt.

On the other hand, Mary fully believed God. Her question was more of a how-to question. How can a virgin give birth? With Zechariah, it wasn't unheard of or unprecedented that an old man could sire a child.

Does that give as much comfort to you as it did to me the first time that I realized what she was asking?

God calls us to lean on the faithfulness that He has proven throughout history while doing new things in our midst currently.

The juxtaposition of Mary and Zechariah shows us how we can walk completely in faith and believe that God will complete what He promises while allowing us the freedom to ask Him how He will do it.

Sometimes He chooses to be clear, encouraging and confirming His plan as He did for Mary (see verses 35–37). Other times, we feel like Sarah or Hannah. The details are left to us to define. Regardless, we can rest assured in the promises of the scripture that confirms the truth: Our God is faithful.

How do you tend to respond when God says something specific to you? Are you skeptical? Do you blow it off? Do you immediately follow through?

_____

_____

_____

_____

Close today by asking God to reveal the places where you are struggling with unbelief. If you are not having doubts, praise Him, in advance, for the things that you know He will do in your life. Above all today, thank Him for being a God who is not afraid of our questions and doubts and who fills us with faith through His Spirit.

New English Translation (NET)

Birth Announcement of Jesus the Messiah

In the sixth month of Elizabeth's pregnancy, the angel Gabriel was sent by God to a town of Galilee called Nazareth, to a virgin engaged to a man whose name was Joseph, a descendant of David, and the virgin's name was Mary. The angel came to her and said, "Greetings, favored one, the Lord is with you!" But she was greatly troubled by his words and began to wonder about the meaning of this greeting. So the angel said to her, "Do not be afraid, Mary, for you have found favor with God! Listen: You will become pregnant and give birth to a son, and you will name him Jesus. He will be great, and will be called the Son of the Most High, and the Lord God will give him the throne of his father David. He will reign over the house of Jacob forever, and his kingdom will never end." Mary said to the angel, "How will this be, since I have not had sexual relations with a man?" The angel replied, "The Holy Spirit will come upon you, and the power of the Most High will overshadow you. Therefore the child to be born will be holy; he will be called the Son of God. And look, your relative Elizabeth has also become pregnant with a son in her old age—although she was called barren, she is now in her sixth month! For nothing will be impossible with God." So Mary said, "Yes, I am a servant of the Lord; let this happen to me according to your word." Then the angel departed from her.

Mary and Elizabeth

In those days Mary got up and went hurriedly into the hill country, to a town of Judah, and entered Zechariah's house and greeted Elizabeth. When Elizabeth heard Mary's greeting, the baby leaped in her womb, and Elizabeth was filled with the Holy Spirit. She exclaimed with a loud voice, "Blessed are you among women, and blessed is the child in your womb! And who am I that the mother of my Lord should come and visit me? For the instant the sound of your greeting reached my ears, the baby in my womb leaped for joy. And blessed is she who believed that what was spoken to her by the Lord would be fulfilled."

Mary's Hymn of Praise

And Mary said, "My soul exalts the Lord, and my spirit has begun to rejoice in God my Savior, because he has looked upon the humble state of his servant. For from now on all generations will call me blessed, because he who is mighty has done great things for me, and holy is his name; from generation to generation he is merciful to those who fear him. He has demonstrated power with his arm; he has scattered those whose pride wells up from the sheer arrogance of their hearts.

He has brought down the mighty from their thrones, and has lifted up those of lowly position; he has filled the hungry with good things, and has sent the rich away empty. He has helped his servant Israel, remembering his mercy, as he promised to our ancestors, to Abraham and to his descendants forever." So Mary stayed with Elizabeth about three months and then returned to her home.

At the end of eight days, when he was circumcised, he was named Jesus, the name given by the angel before he was conceived in the womb.

Jesus' Presentation at the Temple

Now when the time came for their purification according to the law of Moses, Joseph and Mary brought Jesus up to Jerusalem to present him to the Lord (just as it is written in the law of the Lord, "Every firstborn male will be set apart to the Lord"), and to offer a sacrifice according to what is specified in the law of the Lord, a pair of doves or two young pigeons.

The Prophecy of Simeon

Now there was a man in Jerusalem named Simeon who was righteous and devout, looking for the restoration of Israel, and the Holy Spirit was upon him. It had been revealed to him by the Holy Spirit that he would not die before he had seen the Lord's Christ. So Simeon, directed by the Spirit, came into the temple courts, and when the parents brought in the child Jesus to do for him what was customary according to the law, Simeon took him in his arms and blessed God, saying, "Now, according to your word, Sovereign Lord, permit your servant to depart in peace. For my eyes have seen your salvation that you have prepared in the presence of all peoples: a light, for revelation to the Gentiles, and for glory to your people Israel." So the child's father and mother were amazed at what was said about him. Then Simeon blessed them and said to his mother Mary, "Listen carefully: This child is destined to be the cause of the falling and rising of many in Israel and to be a sign that will be rejected. Indeed, as a result of him the thoughts of many hearts will be revealed—and a sword will pierce your own soul as well!" (Luke 1:26–56; 2:21–35)

DAY 2
FAITH ACCEPTS

Ask the Holy Spirit to give you ears to hear, eyes to see, and a heart that is open to His Word. Read Luke 1:26–56 in the text that is provided.

Many questions probably circled in Mary's mind, not because of her lack of faith but because of her wondering, *How on earth will the Holy Spirit place a child in my womb?* Can you imagine how she felt those first few weeks? She would have to wait until her body started to reveal that the most beautiful person to grace the face of the earth was developing in her body.

The pregnancy would have been the epicenter of rippling uncertainty throughout her life. Would her family be ashamed of her pregnancy because she had not been married? Did her community talk behind her back? How would Joseph, her fiancé, respond? Would he divorce her and leave her a widow? During this time in history, a divorced woman was considered a widow by the law, even though her husband was still alive.[12]

Read Matthew 1:18–25 and record how Joseph had to exercise his own faith.

_____

_____

_____

_____

Even with uncertainty churning around her, in advance, Mary resolved to trust that the Lord would do exactly as He had said that He would. This prompted her cousin to exclaim in Luke 1:45,

"_____ is she who has _____ that what the Lord has
_____ to her will be _____." (See also Luke 1:16–38 and
Matthew 1:18–24)

Before her Savior made His way into her arms, her heart
embraced Him, and she worshipped the Lord for, "The Mighty
One has done great things for me" (Luke 1:49).

It's important to believe beforehand that the Lord will finish what He has started. It's crucial that we
embrace the God of the promise more than the promise itself. Mary gives us an incredible example.

Do you remember writing Psalm 27:14? Write it again below and the circumstance of your waiting.
Pray this over your heart.

_____

_____

_____

_____

Here's what I've learned through it all: [Name the circumstance or person]. Don't
give up [name the hope that you have]; don't be impatient [name the time frame];
be entwined as one with the Lord. Be brave and courageous, and never lose hope
[that God can _____]. Yes, keep on waiting—for he will never disappoint you!"
(Psalm 27:14 TPT)

Do you find yourself more focused and excited about what is ahead at the goal versus the here
and now?

_____

_____

_____

_____

Sometimes God gives us these beautiful gifts. Currently in my own life, I am planning to move across the country for no other reason than that God placed a desire in my heart, opened the door, and is beckoning me to trust Him through the entire process. I am not moving for a job, a relationship, or any other sane reason. Literally, I'm moving because God said, *This is what I have for you. Now walk with me.*

I am a planner at heart, and normally, it would be agonizing for me not to be able to plan at this moment. I can't control when a house will be completed. I don't have an official start date with my new job. Therefore, I can't reserve a moving truck, give notice at my current job, put my house on the market, or put a down payment on the new one until I know the unknowns. How much will my house sell for? What if the closing date gets extended? When will I know about the job? All these questions swirl in my mind, and it is incredibly easy to get overwhelmed. So much of it is a mystery!

Yet so much is known. I know that my God is good. I know that He determines my steps and gives wisdom to those who ask. He knows exactly when my house will sell and how much it will sell for. He knows precisely when I will start my new job and what my role will be. He knows how much moving trucks cost, how long it takes to drive from the east to the west, and whether or not my house will be ready when I get there. He is sovereign, and that means if He said it, He will do it. My faith has learned to accept the plans God has for me.

This does not mean that I don't think about and get excited for the future. I do! I am! I cannot wait to see the reason that the Lord is moving me. However, what a shame it would be if I blocked God from it until I got there and then decided to enjoy the new place more than I enjoyed God on the entire journey.

Spirit,

Help me to focus on You rather than on any result today. If I arrive at the end of my journey having missed You on it the whole time, I've missed the entire point of the journey. When my heart is pulled to put all my eggs in the basket of result, reign it in to the step-by-step faith-walk that You have me on and reveal more of Yourself to me. Bring me to the point where I do not even want the result if it means missing You. As Psalm 27:14 says, "Let me be entwined as one with You— You will never disappoint!"

The Message (MSG)

A Virgin Conceives

In the sixth month of Elizabeth's pregnancy, God sent the angel Gabriel to the Galilean village of Nazareth to a virgin engaged to be married to a man descended from David. His name was Joseph, and the virgin's name, Mary. Upon entering, Gabriel greeted her: Good morning! You're beautiful with God's beauty, Beautiful inside and out! God be with you. She was thoroughly shaken, wondering what was behind a greeting like that. But the angel assured her, "Mary, you have nothing to fear. God has a surprise for you: You will become pregnant and give birth to a son and call his name Jesus. He will be great, be called 'Son of the Highest.' The Lord God will give him the throne of his father David; He will rule Jacob's house forever—no end, ever, to his kingdom." Mary said to the angel, "But how? I've never slept with a man." The angel answered, The Holy Spirit will come upon you, the power of the Highest hover over you; Therefore, the child you bring to birth will be called Holy, Son of God. "And did you know that your cousin Elizabeth conceived a son, old as she is? Everyone called her barren, and here she is six months pregnant! Nothing, you see, is impossible with God." And Mary said, Yes, I see it all now: I'm the Lord's maid, ready to serve. Let it be with me just as you say. Then the angel left her.

Blessed Among Women

Mary didn't waste a minute. She got up and traveled to a town in Judah in the hill country, straight to Zachariah's house, and greeted Elizabeth. When Elizabeth heard Mary's greeting, the baby in her womb leaped. She was filled with the Holy Spirit, and sang out exuberantly, You're so blessed among women, and the babe in your womb, also blessed! And why am I so blessed that the mother of my Lord visits me? The moment the sound of your greeting entered my ears, The babe in my womb skipped like a lamb for sheer joy. Blessed woman, who believed what God said, believed every word would come true! And Mary said, I'm bursting with God-news; I'm dancing the song of my Savior God. God took one good look at me, and look what happened—I'm the most fortunate woman on earth! What God has done for me will never be forgotten, the God whose very name is holy, set apart from all others. His mercy flows in wave after wave on those who are in awe before him. He bared his arm and showed his strength, scattered the bluffing braggarts. He knocked tyrants off their high horses, pulled victims out of the mud. The starving poor sat down to a banquet; the callous rich were left out in the cold. He embraced his chosen child, Israel; he remembered and piled on the mercies, piled them high. It's exactly what he promised, beginning with Abraham and right up to now. Mary stayed with Elizabeth for three months and then went back to her own home.

Blessings

When the eighth day arrived, the day of circumcision, the child was named Jesus, the name given by the angel before he was conceived.

Then when the days stipulated by Moses for purification were complete, they took him up to Jerusalem to offer him to God as commanded in God's Law: "Every male who opens the womb shall be a holy offering to God," and also to sacrifice the "pair of doves or two young pigeons" prescribed in God's Law.

In Jerusalem at the time, there was a man, Simeon by name, a good man, a man who lived in the prayerful expectancy of help for Israel. And the Holy Spirit was on him. The Holy Spirit had shown him that he would see the Messiah of God before he died. Led by the Spirit, he entered the Temple. As the parents of the child Jesus brought him in to carry out the rituals of the Law, Simeon took him into his arms and blessed God: God, you can now release your servant; release me in peace as you promised. With my own eyes I've seen your salvation; it's now out in the open for everyone to see: A God-revealing light to the non-Jewish nations, and of glory for your people Israel. Jesus' father and mother were speechless with surprise at these words. Simeon went on to bless them, and said to Mary his mother, This child marks both the failure and the recovery of many in Israel, A figure misunderstood and contradicted—the pain of a sword-thrust through you—But the rejection will force honesty, as God reveals who they really are. (Luke 1:26-56, 2:21-35).

DAY 3

FAITH ANTICIPATES

Ask the Holy Spirit to give you ears to hear, eyes to see, and a heart that is open to His Word. Read Luke 2:1–7 and 21–35 in the text that is provided.

As Joseph and Mary were doing what was required of the law, *the time came* for Jesus to enter the world. But the arrival of Jesus did not mean that Mary's waiting was over. When Jesus was just eight days old, Simeon, a man who had been waiting on a promise from God, blessed the child and gave a pronouncement in verse 34. What did he say?

_____

_____

_____

_____

And a sword will pierce your own soul too.

Wait, what? No, that's not how it's supposed to be! Why does this seem to be an unfair result?

_____

_____

_____

_____

Mary had been faithful. Couldn't she just have lived out her days in harmony and in the favor of God? Why was pain involved when she so willingly believed God and did everything asked of her? Because, my friend, God is not a you-scratch-My-back-I'll-scratch-yours type of God. What goes around does *not* always come back around.

While that may be initially disappointing, it is actually the most beautiful and essential element of our relationship with Christ. Grace is what sets followers of the Way apart from every other religion on the planet.

Have you ever experienced being faithful yet ending up on the other side of pain?

_____

_____

_____

_____

As thrilled as Mary was to hear confirmation that her son was the salvation of her people, there had to be a pang in her heart as she listened to a righteous man proclaiming that there would be pain and strife to come. Liefeld and Pao stated,

> There will be a cost to Jesus. As the one who himself is the ultimate "sign," the visible affirmation of God's declared intentions, he will be vulnerable to the hostility of unbelievers. A negative attitude toward him, however, serves to brand the unbeliever as one who has rejected not only him but also the whole of God's revelation. This clash will inevitably wound Jesus' mother.[13]

Look up John 16:31–33.

What does Jesus tell them to anticipate?

_____

_____

_____

_____

What does Jesus promise them?

_____

_____

_____

_____

Is it easier to worship the fact that in Jesus we are more than conquerors or to worship Jesus, who has made us more than conquerors? (See Romans 8:37) Do we worship the gift or the gift giver? Do we worship the result or the One determining results?

_____

_____

_____

_____

There will be a cost.

Mary had to watch her son be rejected and despised. She watched as her child suffered a criminal's death. She had to endure hearing the insults that were hurled at her son. The hardest part for me to grasp is that she knew that He did not deserve this and that He was the Son of God.

What circumstance are you facing that you know is ultimately right but is going to cause you pain?

_____

_____

_____

_____

There will always be a cost. What has waiting cost you?

_____

_____

_____

_____

Reminisce with God about the cost of waiting. What has it cost Him? What has it cost you?

New Living Translation (NLT)

The Birth of Jesus Foretold

In the sixth month of Elizabeth's pregnancy, God sent the angel Gabriel to Nazareth, a village in Galilee, to a virgin named Mary. She was engaged to be married to a man named Joseph, a descendant of King David. Gabriel appeared to her and said, "Greetings, favored woman! The Lord is with you!" Confused and disturbed, Mary tried to think what the angel could mean. "Don't be afraid, Mary," the angel told her, "for you have found favor with God! You will conceive and give birth to a son, and you will name him Jesus. He will be very great and will be called the Son of the Most High. The Lord God will give him the throne of his ancestor David. And he will reign over Israel forever; his Kingdom will never end!" Mary asked the angel, "But how can this happen? I am a virgin." The angel replied, "The Holy Spirit will come upon you, and the power of the Most High will overshadow you. So the baby to be born will be holy, and he will be called the Son of God. What's more, your relative Elizabeth has become pregnant in her old age! People used to say she was barren, but she has conceived a son and is now in her sixth month. For the word of God will never fail." Mary responded, "I am the Lord's servant. May everything you have said about me come true." And then the angel left her.

Mary Visits Elizabeth

A few days later Mary hurried to the hill country of Judea, to the town where Zechariah lived. She entered the house and greeted Elizabeth. At the sound of Mary's greeting, Elizabeth's child leaped within her, and Elizabeth was filled with the Holy Spirit. Elizabeth gave a glad cry and exclaimed to Mary, "God has blessed you above all women, and your child is blessed. Why am I so honored, that the mother of my Lord should visit me? When I heard your greeting, the baby in my womb jumped for joy. You are blessed because you believed that the Lord would do what he said."

The Magnificat: Mary's Song of Praise

Mary responded, "Oh, how my soul praises the Lord. How my spirit rejoices in God my Savior! For he took notice of his lowly servant girl, and from now on all generations will call me blessed. For the Mighty One is holy, and he has done great things for me. He shows mercy from generation to generation to all who fear him. His mighty arm has done tremendous things! He has scattered the proud and haughty ones. He has brought down princes from their thrones and exalted the humble. He has filled the hungry with good things and sent the rich away with empty hands. He has helped his servant Israel and remembered to be merciful. For he made this promise to our ancestors, to Abraham and his children forever." Mary stayed with Elizabeth about three months and then went back to her own home.

Jesus Is Presented in the Temple

Eight days later, when the baby was circumcised, he was named Jesus, the name given him by the angel even before he was conceived. Then it was time for their purification offering, as required by the law of Moses after the birth of a child; so his parents took him to Jerusalem to present him to the Lord. The law of the Lord says, "If a woman's first child is a boy, he must be dedicated to the Lord." So they offered the sacrifice required in the law of the Lord—"either a pair of turtledoves or two young pigeons."

The Prophecy of Simeon

At that time there was a man in Jerusalem named Simeon. He was righteous and devout and was eagerly waiting for the Messiah to come and rescue Israel. The Holy Spirit was upon him and had revealed to him that he would not die until he had seen the Lord's Messiah. That day the Spirit led him to the Temple. So when Mary and Joseph came to present the baby Jesus to the Lord as the law required, Simeon was there. He took the child in his arms and praised God, saying, "Sovereign Lord, now let your servant die in peace, as you have promised. I have seen your salvation, which you have prepared for all people. He is a light to reveal God to the nations, and he is the glory of your people Israel!" Jesus' parents were amazed at what was being said about him. Then Simeon blessed them, and he said to Mary, the baby's mother, "This child is destined to cause many in Israel to fall, and many others to rise. He has been sent as a sign from God, but many will oppose him. As a result, the deepest thoughts of many hearts will be revealed. And a sword will pierce your very soul." (Luke 1:26–56; 2:21–35)

DAY 4

FAITH RESOLVES

Ask the Holy Spirit to give you ears to hear, eyes to see, and a heart that is open to His Word. Read Luke 2:21–35.

Mary had no idea when Simeon's prophecies were going to take place or what they would look like. She had to wait for God's plan to unfold. Even still, Mary trusted God with her heart. Despite agonizing seasons of waiting, her faithfulness was breathtaking. She had to wait during her pregnancy for Jesus to be born. She had to wait and watch His life as He did exactly as His Father had commanded Him to do. She had to wait for Him to be arrested, to be tried, to be beaten, to be nailed to a cross, and to die for the sins of the world.

Then in the way that only she could experience it, she had to wait three excruciating days in the unknown, following Jesus's crucifixion. What had happened? He was supposed to be the Messiah! She knew that she had carried the miracle in her womb. She had watched the wonders that He had performed with her own eyes. Her faith was resolved. When had God ever let her down before?

When have you felt like all was lost?

_____

_____

_____

_____

How are we pulled into acting like we are mourning without hope (see 1 Thessalonians 4:13)?

_____

_____

_____

_____

Read any one of the following: Matthew 28:1–10, Mark 16, Luke 24, or John 20.

Jesus rose again when *the time was right,* according to the Father's will. We will always have seasons of waiting. God has established an undeniable rhythm in life. As soon as one season ends, another begins.

For example, you could look at the story of God like the seasons of a year. The Old Testament is like summer. Everything started with perfect, full blooms of life, which ended up in a hot and scorched land that was aching for a Savior. The New Testament is like autumn. It reveals its beauty in the midst of dying leaves, just as Jesus came and died for the sin of the world.

We are currently living in winter. The church is established and growing, but it's hard. There is a constant headwind, hearts are cold, and everything feels harder than it should. But soon it will be spring, and we will all be raised and joined together with Christ to begin our new lives in God's presence forever. All will be set right. There will be no more fighting, striving, toiling, hurting … and no more waiting. Whether we are on this earth or not, our waiting *will* end. But while we are on this earth, let's choose to respond in a way that glorifies God and recognize that we can always trust Him because He is more than faithful.

What season do you find yourself in?

_____

_____

_____

_____

What season are you experiencing in your church body?

_____

_____

_____

_____

Do you agree that the global church is in a winter?

_____

_____

_____

_____

Let's explore more. What do we have to look forward to when all our seasons of waiting have ended? Write what each verse reveals.

Revelation 4:8, 11 (What are the creatures and elders saying nonstop?)

_____

_____

_____

_____

Revelation 5:9–13 (Who is their worship focused on?)

_____

_____

_____

_____

Revelation 19:11–16 (How is Jesus described?)

_____

_____

_____

_____

Revelation 21:3–5 (What does God promise in eternity?)

_____

_____

_____

_____

Revelation 21:6-7 (How does God describe Himself?)

_____

_____

_____

_____

Revelation 21:23–24 (What is the role of light in eternity?)

_____

_____

_____

_____

Revelation 22 tells us, "These words are trustworthy and true" (verse 6). Three times Jesus says, "I am coming soon!" (verses 7, 12, and 20). Can you even imagine that?

In these bitter, uncomfortable, and hard-pressed days, I thank God that I can join creation in worshipping Him. Worship goes on 24-7 before Him. He is faithful and true, and His glory is beyond description.

Tears, pain, and heartache will be wiped away. My time on earth may end, but the One who determines my days is the Alpha and Omega. I'll be with Him forever. His glory will be so bright that there will be no need for the sun. The true light will be shining!

Thank God for His sacrifice and resurrection. Ask Him to give you patience as we await His return.

New American Standard Bible (NASB)

Jesus' Birth Foretold

Now in the sixth month the angel Gabriel was sent from God to a city in Galilee called Nazareth, to a virgin engaged to a man whose name was Joseph, of the descendants of David; and the virgin's name was Mary. And coming in, he said to her, "Greetings, favored one! The Lord is with you." But she was very perplexed at this statement, and kept pondering what kind of salutation this was. The angel said to her, "Do not be afraid, Mary; for you have found favor with God. And behold, you will conceive in your womb and bear a son, and you shall name Him Jesus. He will be great and will be called the Son of the Most High; and the Lord God will give Him the throne of His father David; and He will reign over the house of Jacob forever, and His kingdom will have no end." Mary said to the angel, "How can this be, since I am a virgin?" The angel answered and said to her, "The Holy Spirit will come upon you, and the power of the Most High will overshadow you; and for that reason the holy Child shall be called the Son of God. And behold, even your relative Elizabeth has also conceived a son in her old age; and she who was called barren is now in her sixth month. For nothing will be impossible with God." And Mary said, "Behold, the bondslave of the Lord; may it be done to me according to your word." And the angel departed from her.

Mary Visits Elizabeth

Now at this time Mary arose and went in a hurry to the hill country, to a city of Judah, and entered the house of Zacharias and greeted Elizabeth. When Elizabeth heard Mary's greeting, the baby leaped in her womb; and Elizabeth was filled with the Holy Spirit. And she cried out with a loud voice and said, "Blessed are you among women, and blessed is the fruit of your womb! And how has it happened to me, that the mother of my Lord would come to me? For behold, when the sound of your greeting reached my ears, the baby leaped in my womb for joy. And blessed is she who believed that there would be a fulfillment of what had been spoken to her by the Lord."

The Magnificat

And Mary said: "My soul exalts the Lord, And my spirit has rejoiced in God my Savior. For He has had regard for the humble state of His bondslave; For behold, from this time on all generations will count me blessed. For the Mighty One has done great things for me; And holy is His name. And His mercy is upon generation after generation toward those who fear Him. He has done mighty deeds with His arm; He has scattered those who were proud in the thoughts of their heart. He has brought down rulers from their thrones, And has exalted those who were humble.

He has filled the hungry with good things; And sent away the rich empty-handed. He has given help to Israel His servant, In remembrance of His mercy, As He spoke to our fathers, to Abraham and his descendants forever." And Mary stayed with her about three months, and then returned to her home.

Jesus Presented at the Temple

And when eight days had passed, before His circumcision, His name was then called Jesus, the name given by the angel before He was conceived in the womb. And when the days for their purification according to the law of Moses were completed, they brought Him up to Jerusalem to present Him to the Lord (as it is written in the Law of the Lord, "Every firstborn male that opens the womb shall be called holy to the Lord"), and to offer a sacrifice according to what was said in the Law of the Lord, "A pair of turtledoves or two young pigeons." And there was a man in Jerusalem whose name was Simeon; and this man was righteous and devout, looking for the consolation of Israel; and the Holy Spirit was upon him. And it had been revealed to him by the Holy Spirit that he would not see death before he had seen the Lord's Christ. And he came in the Spirit into the temple; and when the parents brought in the child Jesus, to carry out for Him the custom of the Law, then he took Him into his arms, and blessed God, and said, "Now Lord, You are releasing Your bond-servant to depart in peace, According to Your word; For my eyes have seen Your salvation, Which You have prepared in the presence of all peoples, A Light of revelation to the Gentiles, And the glory of Your people Israel." And His father and mother were amazed at the things which were being said about Him. And Simeon blessed them and said to Mary His mother, "Behold, this Child is appointed for the fall and rise of many in Israel, and for a sign to be opposed—and a sword will pierce even your own soul—to the end that thoughts from many hearts may be revealed." (Luke 1:26–56; 2:21–35)

DAY 5

FAITH SUBMITS

Ask the Holy Spirit to give you ears to hear, eyes to see, and a heart that is open to His Word. Read Luke 1:26–56 in the text that is provided.

What spiritual blessing is found in Mary's example of waiting? By God's grace, she was highly favored, but her submission to God's plans for her life led her on a journey that no one else would have the opportunity to experience fully. She had the honor of being used in a mighty way because of her trust in Him. In moments that were eclipsed by the unknown, Mary chose to step toward her Father in faith, even though she could not see what was ahead.

She did not allow the season of waiting to be a source of anxiety and fear. Instead, she allowed the season to bring forth a harvest of faithfulness.

The Lord does not desire for us to live in constant confusion or worry. He does desire for us to be in a close relationship with Him, allowing Him to guide our thoughts each day. Read the following and take hold of the promise in this passage.

Read Isaiah 26:3–4 and record the promises our Father gives us.

_____

_____

_____

_____

There are subtle connections between Hannah, Sarah, and Mary. What did the angel ask Sarah in Genesis 18:14?

_____

_____

_____

_____

How did the angel answer Mary's question in Luke 1:37?

_____

_____

_____

_____

It's as if the angel asked Sarah, "Is anything too hard for the Lord?" so that he could answer the question when he declared to Mary, "For nothing is impossible with God." Both Hannah and Mary worshipped the Lord. In fact, Mary's song in Luke 1:46–55 has notable similarities to Hannah's Prayer in 1 Samuel 2:1–10. Mary was a faithful servant just like Hannah was. One commentary notes,

> Her servanthood is not a cringing slavery but a submission to God that in OT times characterized genuine believers and that should characterize believers today. Understandably, Mary doubtless felt empathy with Hannah's sense of being at the Lord's disposal in a part of life over which a woman before modern times had little or no control. Mary's trusting submission at this point in her life may be compared with her attitude toward her son later on.[14]

The point is that Mary submitted to what the Lord was going to do, even if she did not understand the whole story. This isn't a sad thought. She didn't think, *Woe is me because I have no choice in the matter. God's going to do what He wants anyway.* We always have a choice in our response. Isn't the point to be so submitted to God that even in the seasons of waiting, we can trust fully that God is at work. Even though it can be uncertain and painful, He will prove to be a faithful Father.

Are you fighting God's call for your life or submitting to the knowledge that God is sovereign and in control?

_____

_____

_____

_____

See what these verses have to say about submission.
Job 22:21

_____

_____

_____

_____

Psalm 37:5

_____

_____

_____

_____

Proverbs 16:3

_____

_____

_____

_____

Fall under God's authority willingly, and it will go well for you, it may not be by your own definition, but your plans will be established. God loves you too much to give you everything you want and the way you want it, but He will give you what you need.

Father,

If You've deemed this season of waiting to be good for me, help me to trust that it is.

WEEK 4

ANNA

Waiting in the Midst of Upheaval

Science is an amazing thing. It's not something that believers need to fear. More and more, science is catching up with the things that the Bible has been proclaiming all along.

Studies show that changing the way we think greatly affects our responses. Personally, I love this! It makes sense to a believer. Philippians 4:8 comes to mind. Go and look it up. It's worth it.

We are surrounded by a culture that is getting pretty dicey. A lot of what we are told to think and accept can produce all sorts of conflict in our souls. Even if you're not a believer, the world can feel like it's in a constant state of chaos.

Here is a simple example. I have to sleep with my phone in another room. This forces me to wake up, put my feet on the ground, and get in God's Word before I can check notifications, emails, or the news. On days that I do choose to check those things before spending time with my Father, like clockwork, my mind is consumed with those things all day long. If I start in the Word, the first thing that is going into my mind, which I will dwell on all day, is His faithfulness, sovereignty, goodness, and forgiveness.

If we're not careful, we will allow the world to discourage us and steal our hope. Again, this is when Philippians 4:8 is a great encouragement.

What if God is trying to show us that *how* and *what* we think can have a huge impact on the way that we can live more abundantly? Just as we have learned that hope, words, and faith matter, our mindset does too. Let this week's message encourage you to live above the instability around us.

DAY 1

THE AWARE MINDSET

Ask the Holy Spirit to give you ears to hear, eyes to see, and a heart that is open to His Word. Read Luke 2:36–38 in your own Bible.

There is little known about Anna the prophetess, but her place in history gives us great insight into waiting during the seasons of political, cultural, and spiritual upheaval. That's something that we know a lot about in our present-day situation.

Is there part of you that hates feeling as if everything is headed the wrong direction (further from the gospel)? One human viciously attacks another, and then the other person gives a belligerent rebuttal. The truth of God's Word is twisted just enough to justify open sin. The decline of virtues pervades every street and corner of our culture and society.

This is the reason that we need to know everything that we can about Anna the prophetess. She felt these things too. She knew what it felt like to live in a culture that had been taken over by another empire. She was well acquainted with loss. She knew about being demeaned as a person.

She also knew God, and she was trusted by God.

She was a prophetess. This meant that she was chosen by God to carry a specific message and proclaim it. Prophets never carry a minor message. Any time the God of the Universe speaks to His creation, it is always a major message.

Generally speaking, prophets lived harder lives than most did, and Anna was no exception. While there are just three verses concerning her in the Bible, there *are* three verses. Because all scripture is God-breathed, we know that those three verses were written with a purpose, and truly, there is much to glean from this beautiful woman's life.

Read Luke 2:36–38. Write down the facts about who Anna was.

_____

_____

_____

_____

Write down what Anna did.

_____

_____

_____

_____

Write down where Anna's story takes place.

_____

_____

_____

_____

Write about the time in history when Anna lived. Write about her being mentioned in the larger story.

_____

_____

_____

_____

Write down why Anna is found in this scripture.

_____

_____

_____

_____

How did answering the above go? Was it smooth sailing until you got to the *why*?

This week, we will discover more about the heart of Anna and the way that she stood firm in the Lord in the middle of a world that was in upheaval. When studying scripture, the who, what, where, when, and why questions are always a great place to start. Sometimes the meaning is very straightforward, and other times, you have to dig deeper. Digging is the place where the fun is.

As we become aware of Anna's story, find your place too. Your story is being written as well. A lot of good can come from knowing ourselves. This may seem like a silly or simple exercise, but do it anyway. For example, don't answer the question, where are you? by giving your city and state. This is more than an introduction to a stranger. This is about becoming aware of who you are at the core.

Who are you? (nurturer, caregiver, fighter, avoider, pleaser, etc.)

_____

_____

_____

_____

What do you do? (care for people, push people away, fight for justice, bring out the best in others, etc.)

_____

_____

_____

_____

Where are you? (lost, on a mountaintop, confused, satisfied, etc.)

_____

_____

_____

_____

When did you find yourself there? (constant struggle, in the past 5 years, revealed yesterday, etc.)

_____

_____

_____

_____

Why are you here on this Earth?

_____

_____

_____

_____

Take time to pray that the Holy Spirit will reveal whom He is and the way that He wants to use of Anna's life to impact your time of waiting.

New American Standard Bible (NASB)

And there was a prophetess, Anna the daughter of Phanuel, of the tribe of Asher. She was advanced in years and had lived with her husband seven years after her marriage, and then as a widow to the age of eighty-four. She never left the temple, serving night and day with fasting and prayers. At that very moment she came up and began giving thanks to God, and continued to speak of Him to all those who were looking for the redemption of Jerusalem. (Luke 2:36–38)

DAY 2

THE PREPARED MINDSET

Ask the Holy Spirit to give you ears to hear, eyes to see, and a heart that is open to His Word. Read Luke 2:36–38 in the text that is provided.

Luke reveals to his readers that Anna was a _____, the daughter of _____, born of the tribe of _____ and had been _____ seven short years after her marriage began. She was at least eighty-four years old (possibly older) and devoted herself to _____ , _____, and _____ at the temple. She had experienced what Sarah, Hannah, and Mary had not. She had experienced loss and loneliness, and she was without the physical companionship of a husband or family to lean on.

Let's note what Anna had done with the life that God given her. The text does not say that she became bitter or self-focused. She didn't develop a victim mentality, wondering what she had done to deserve losing her husband at a young age and not having children. In fact, it says the very opposite. It says that she spent her life in worship, prayer, and fasting. She was preparing.

Because of her constant awareness and preparedness, Anna
was privy to something most that people missed.

Prayer is such a gift. How kind is it that God allows us to bend His ear? Not only that, but He also leans down and speaks into our ears? He longs for us to know His heart.

Read and meditate on Psalm 116:1–2. Read it in multiple translations. The New Living Translation and the Amplified Version have spoken to my heart again and again. Write these two verses below in your own words.

_____

_____

_____

_____

Fasting is also an often overlooked and misunderstood gift. Fasting is not twisting the arm of God or doing something hard in order to get something from Him. Of all the spiritual disciplines, this one is far harder to fully embrace than reading your Bible, praying, and worshipping God with your life.

Fasting takes the faith that is residing in our hearts and minds and incorporates it into our bodies. By denying your body a legitimate need, you are expressing your need to know God more. More than your body needs food, your soul needs your Father.

Every time I have fasted, I have been impressed by God in some way. By impress, I don't mean, "Whoa, God, what you did there was impressive." Instead, I mean that He left an impression on me. He slowed me down enough to actually hear Him, see Him, and have truth revealed in ways that I would otherwise have missed all together. Take time to fast.

What distractions are you knowingly or unknowingly turning to?

_____

_____

_____

_____

This week, what would you be willing to fast from for a specific amount of time to seek the Lord regarding your wait, if God is lays that on your heart?

_____

_____

_____

_____

How are you preparing your heart and mind to be sensitive to the things that God is doing?

_____

_____

_____

_____

Father,

I live in a world that loves to use distractions to help alleviate pain during times of waiting. Keep me from falling into the trap of distractions. Help me give them up to focus on You. Anna did this, and she was constantly on the lookout for what You were doing. You chose her to tell people about the redemption that was found in Jesus. Let me be ripe for the picking as well.

Amplified Version (AMP)

There was a prophetess, Anna, the daughter of Phanuel, of the tribe of Asher. She was very old, and had lived with her husband for seven years after her marriage, and then as a widow to the age of eighty-four. She did not leave the [area of the] temple, but was serving *and* worshiping night and day with fastings and prayers. She, too, came up at that very moment and *began* praising *and* giving thanks to God, and continued to speak of Him to all who were looking for the redemption *and* deliverance of Jerusalem. (Luke 2:36-38)

DAY 3

THE EXPECTANT MINDSET

Ask the Holy Spirit to give you ears to hear, eyes to see, and a heart that is open to His Word. Read Luke 2:36–38 in the text that is provided.

The statement that Anna "did not depart from the temple" does not necessarily mean that she resided there. It does indicate that it was an acceptable practice for a widow to spend most of her time in the temple, engaged in "fasting and prayers."[15]

What is most of your time spent doing? Where do you mostly reside physically? Where do you mostly reside mentally?

_____

_____

_____

_____

Last week we learned that while Joseph and Mary were doing what was required by Jewish law (presenting Jesus at the temple), Simeon prophesied concerning Jesus. *"Coming up to them at that very moment*, Anna gave thanks to God and spoke about the child" (Luke 2:38). The beauty of the timing in this moment cannot be ignored. I love the phrases in the Bible that clue us in. This was a holy moment. Anna did not come running up before Simeon had spoken or five minutes after that but right as it was happening. With so many years of longing for the Messiah between them, I wonder if she and Simeon looked at each other in astonishment, screaming, "Can you believe this?"

What was Anna's first response?

_____

_____

_____

_____

She gave thanks. She worshipped. Have you noticed her automatic responses? She spent time in the presence of the Lord. She kept herself in a posture of giving and receiving. She kept the lines of communication open. She honored the rituals that showed devotion to her God. Since worship was her lifestyle, what she did was intended to bring glory to God. When she lived like that, it's no wonder that the first words out of her mouth were ones of gratitude.

She had cultivated gratitude as her native tongue.

Look at the following verses and record the common theme in them.

Job 6:10

_____

_____

_____

_____

Psalm 31:7

_____

_____

_____

_____

Psalm 40:16

_____

_____

_____

_____

Psalm 118:24

_____

_____

_____

_____

Isaiah 49:13

_____

_____

_____

_____

Philippians 1:18

_____

_____

_____

_____

1 Peter 1:6–8

_____

_____

_____

_____

I hope that you can see in these verses that we are called to rejoice, not only when everything is going well but also when things have been going poorly because of a change in circumstances. We are to worship *always*.

Paul tells us in Philippians 4:4, "Rejoice in the Lord always; again I will say, rejoice." In a separate letter, he doubles down and says, "Rejoice always" (1Thessalonians 5:16, 18). Do you think these people were living their best days? No way! When Paul was writing to the church at Philippi, he was in prison. When he wrote to Thessalonica, he encouraged a young church to stay the course in the face of cults and idolatry.

You will never go wrong when you respond in worship. When you worship, you bring glory to God while calling yourself to remember all the reasons that you love and serve Him. You are expectant that He will prove to be mighty and powerful through your testimony. You serve a saving, righteous, holy, and faithful God. He is the God who looks at your hurts and longings and turns them into the backdrop of His beautiful story—a story full of everlasting fulfillment, which is found in Him.

Are you tired of being single? That doesn't take away your ability to praise God. Are you sitting in the worst loss of your life? That doesn't take away your ability to praise God. Is your marriage falling apart? That doesn't take away your ability to praise God. Has there been infertility, death, sickness, mental illness, or confusion? As long as there is a heart beating in your chest, nothing can take away your ability to worship God. When you least "feel" like worshipping, that's often when it is the most healing. Raise your expectancy so that you don't miss what God is doing on a greater scale.

We are living in very real and trying times. Through loss, struggles, and devastation, which you feel are unique to you, God graciously allows you to know Him in a way that very few people can understand. I am not saying that the change of mindset happens easily or overnight. A supernatural thing must take place.

A few years ago and months after a relationship had not worked out, my mentor asked me, "Have you thanked God for this?"

Have I thanked God for it not working out? I thought. *Have I thanked God that I spent years believing I heard Him clearly regarding this relationship? Have I thanked God for putting my faith on the line and my now feeling like people looked at me as if I was a fool? Have I thanked God for believing in Him over and over, yet I was the one who was let down?* No, I hadn't thanked God.

That night, we had a large choir rehearsal where our entire worship team came together to learn new songs for an upcoming conference. I found myself on my knees, exhausted from holding God responsible for my heartache. I wept and repented for withholding my gratitude and worship in an effort to desire a different outcome.

Years later, I can say that I get over matters of the heart not working out *much quicker* than I used to because of what I learned during that time. Believe it or not, people understand when I say, "It didn't turn out the way I wanted it to. I still can't explain why God called me to believe Him so fervently for that relationship. But I do know this: my faith is stronger because of it. Even though I don't possess what I thought was a promise from Him, I know to my core that God is faithful. I am so thankful He chose me to go through that." God honors our faith.

How do you develop deeper trust when it doesn't work out? Are you withholding your worship from God because of a circumstance? If so, you can use this as a model when you pray.

Father,

I hate that _____.

But I will praise You anyway.

Then list His attributes. Write out the reasons that you're thankful. Make a playlist of songs about worshipping God when it's hard.

Spend some time worshipping God.

New English Translation (NET Bible)

The Testimony of Anna

There was also a prophetess, Anna the daughter of Phanuel, of the tribe of Asher. She was very old, having been married to her husband for seven years until his death. She had lived as a widow since then for eighty-four years. She never left the temple, worshiping with fasting and prayer night and day. At that moment, she came up to them and began to give thanks to God and to speak about the child to all who were waiting for the redemption of Jerusalem. (Luke 2:36–38)

DAY 4

THE STEADFAST MINDSET

Ask the Holy Spirit to give you ears to hear, eyes to see, and a heart that is open to His Word. Read Luke 2:36–38 in the text that is provided.

Anna lived during the Pax Romana, the historical two hundred years of peace and stability within the Roman Empire under the powerful rule of Augustus.[16] Sure, times seemed peaceful to those in authority; however, that did not negate the fact that she was a widowed Jewish woman waiting for the redemption of her people, land, and status. As Simeon pointed to the salvation of Israel, Anna looked "forward to the redemption of Jerusalem" (Luke 2:38). She had been waiting her entire life for the redemption of her people and land. Above all, she had been patiently waiting for the promised Messiah.

Anna knew the promises of God. She was familiar with the prophecies of old. She knew the very land that her feet stood on, under the rule of an outside authority, would be returned to her people. She knew that God had chosen the Israelites as His own even though the Israelites were not respected by other nations. Despite the fact that this society didn't value women beyond childbearing, she knew that she was created in the image of God, and therefore, she had intrinsic value.

What are you waiting to be redeemed? Is it your reputation? Is it your body? Is it your family?

_____

_____

_____

_____

The Greek word used in Luke 2:38 for *redemption* is *lutrosis*,[17] which comes from the root word *luo*.[18] In the spiritual sense, we tie redemption *(lutrosis)* to a taking back of land or people, paying a ransom, or delivery out of sin. Another definition given for *luo* is "to loose one bound, i.e. to unbind, release from bonds, set free."

Anna declared Jesus as the redemption of her people. In essence, she was saying that Jesus was bringing the freedom of her people.

> *She waited her whole life for freedom, and now, here*
> *was her answer right before her very eyes.*

Read John 8:36, 2 Corinthians 3:17, and Galatians 5:1 and write the common theme below.

_____

_____

_____

_____

If we are in Christ, we are free indeed and graced to live out this reality every day. Our circumstances do not own us. Our relationships do not own us. What we have and do not have does not hold ownership over us. The only thing that we are mastered by is the Master.

This, my friend, is where the waiting becomes worth it. In her upside-down world, Anna was set free while she was waiting. She did not have to solve the earth's problems. She did not have to fight to be taken seriously. She did not have to shoulder the responsibility of making everything work out perfectly.

Do you know what she did have to do? She had to wait on what she knew was true. She had to trust that her God was working in the days that He seemed distant and silent. She had to devote herself to seeking God and consistently worshipping Him. She had to believe that the time she spent in the in-between, with the hurt and loss, was preparation for something greater that was coming. In that place—the process of day in, day out, and endless hours-she was set free. She handed over all she could not do to the One who could do it all.

I want to wait like that. In my circumstances, I want to wait with the hope and expectation that freedom affords me. In my everyday life, I want my heart, mind, and body to start catching up with the freedom that my soul has in Christ. I want bad habits to die and healthy habits to form. I want to take what I've been given and let God rule over every ounce of it. I want to see my selfish desires decreasing and the Spirit's desires increasing in my life and the church. The freedom comes in knowing that I am not in control.

Using the definition of being set free, what needs to be redeemed in your life?

_____

_____

_____

_____

In what ways can you see God using your season of waiting to bring freedom to your life?

_____

_____

_____

_____

Use the rest of this page to record all the things that you have been set free from and are now free to do. Look at your who, what, where, when, and why answers on Day 1 and see if that gives you any further insight to areas that need redemption.

The Message (MSG)

Anna the prophetess was also there, a daughter of Phanuel from the tribe of Asher. She was by now a very old woman. She had been married seven years and a widow for eighty-four. She never left the Temple area, worshiping night and day with her fasting and prayers. At the very time Simeon was praying, she showed up, broke into an anthem of praise to God, and talked about the child to all who were waiting expectantly for the freeing of Jerusalem. (Luke 2:36–38

DAY 5

THE WARRIOR MINDSET

Ask the Holy Spirit to give you ears to hear, eyes to see, and a heart that is open to His Word. Read Luke 2:36–38 in the text that is provided.

What spiritual benefit can we find in Anna's story?

There is power in hope.

Luke gives the details of Anna's long life as a widow. Perhaps it was "to suggest that the waiting, and the certainty of an eventual reward, has kept her alive."[19]

Anna used her season of waiting to press deeper into a hopeful prayer life that was filled with worship and fasting. Instead of becoming bitter over the political climate and her own under-appreciated social status as a widow with seemingly nothing to offer, she had a perspective that the world was bigger than herself and her own standing. As a result, God used her to help others see Jesus. She was constantly and intentionally looking for the Messiah. When she saw her Savior face-to-face, she did her part to point others to Him as well.

Do you identify with Anna? Do you feel under-appreciated because of your status or situation, even though you have much to offer?

_____

_____

_____

_____

Sometimes do you find that you disregard another person because, in your humanity, you haven't assigned value to someone because of their ability or inability to meet your needs? This tough question requires honesty and humility. Ask God to search your heart and show you the steps that you need to take to confront any thoughts or actions that do not honor others.

_____

_____

_____

_____

Eternity rests in the balance of our willingness to reach out to people. Yes, the Holy Spirit is ultimately responsible for changing the hearts of others and bringing them to Himself, but God chooses to use *us* in that process. We all have relationships and opportunities where we can be Jesus to others.

The challenge for us is to become diligent in seeking them out, to be as attentive as Anna was, and to expect that God will provide these connections if we ask Him. So today, boldly ask God how you can use your life to bring Jesus to others.

In what ways are you using your life to point others to Jesus? Are you diligently looking for opportunities?

_____

_____

_____

_____

We are called to be warriors for we are constantly in a battle. Even if it feels hopeless, we know that it is not.

Read Ephesians 6:10–20. Who are we really at war with?

_____

_____

_____

_____

What action words can you find in verse 13?

_____

_____

_____

_____

Name the pieces of armor, found in verses 14–17, that we are to put on.

_____

_____

_____

_____

What are we told to do in verses 18–20?

_____

_____

_____

_____

With confidence, I believe that although Anna came before Paul, who wrote Ephesians, she was a warrior in every way that was stated earlier. She knew that her enemy was not a person or a system. It was in the spiritual realms and playing out in the hearts of the people who were in a system that considered her worthless. She took her place, resisted evil, and prepared to take a stand. She put on her armor, and her faith was active. She prayed, prayed, and prayed, and she got to see Jesus.

Jesus,

Help me to pursue peace and hope as I wait for You. You know my circumstances, but You also know the plans that You have for me. Help me to not lose myself in my social standing, culture, society, or own tunnel-vision version of life. Burn Your Word into my heart and bring it to my mouth repeatedly.

I lack nothing in You. You esteem me as Your precious and dearly loved daughter. Give me the words to proclaim Your great love to whomever You put in my path and the boldness to share Your gospel. Keep me close to Your heart. Prompt me to communicate with You constantly and to deny myself anything that distracts me from You. Like Anna, help me to hope in the promise of Your return and the setting of all things right. Until then, You will find me at Your feet. Amen.

WEEK 5

MARY AND MARTHA
Waiting in the Midst of Loss

We have all been hurt. We've all had to face a loss of some sort. Depending on what's lost, it may be the hardest circumstance that someone faces. In those moments when we don't understand or feel slighted by God, what we really want is comfort. We want to know the reason why it had to happen. At its worst, a person with this sort of pain is looking for something or someone to blame. Bitterness and resentment can plant a seed as expectations go unmet.

Mary and Martha faced a debilitating loss when their brother, Lazarus, died. Who would take care of them? How could Jesus ignore them when they had rushed to get word to Him? Have you felt like the loss could take you out too? Have you felt let down and disappointed?

However, the sisters possessed something that made the world stare are them in wonder: belief. It was not only belief in an act but also belief in a person. This week, we will learn the role of belief in our lives and the way that it impacts others.

DAY 1

DISAPPOINTED BELIEF

Ask the Holy Spirit to give you ears to hear, eyes to see, and a heart that is open to His Word. Read John 11:1–44 in your own Bible.

Few stories are better known in the Bible than the raising of Lazarus from the dead. The Gospel of John unpacks the story about Lazarus being sick and his sisters, Mary and Martha, sending for Jesus. "The sisters assumed, because of the Lord's ability and His love for Lazarus, that He would immediately respond to their word about Lazarus' illness and come."[20]

Jesus was less than two miles away, and He surely would have been able to make the walk, come, and heal His friend.[21] But Jesus chose to wait. He did not rush to Lazarus and keep His friend from the grip of death. By the time Jesus arrived at friends' home, Lazarus had been in the grave for four days. Read that again.

Death is so final on Earth. Lazarus was not going to come back from it. He had been physically dead for _____ days. I call this disappointed belief.

At times, have you been sure that God was going to show up and reverse the situation, but He seemingly didn't? If so, write it about it. I know that sometimes it's easier to only think about these things, but the act of writing it down forces us to articulate and cement those thoughts. This is part of your story, and it will be used for God's glory, so take the time. It will be well worth it!

_____

_____

_____

_____

The sisters each responded in their own way, which went with their temperaments and personalities. Jesus does not show preference to one over the other. He simply addresses both of them in their grief and need.

Martha runs out to greet Jesus and immediately confesses that if Jesus had been there, her brother would not have died. He encourages her by gently reminding her of who He is. Thereby, He prompts Martha to make her own confession. Then He asks for Mary. When He calls her, she comes quickly to Him, falls at His feet, and states the same words that her sister stated. He is moved with compassion for them, weeps, goes to the tomb, and calls Lazarus to come out. Lazarus walks out of the grave.

We will address the I Am statement of Jesus tomorrow, but before we get there, let's notice something. Both Martha and Mary said the same thing to Jesus: If "You had been here." Jesus replies, "I am" (John 11:25). Read that last sentence aloud, if it will help you understand the full impact of His answer. The way John records it is that Martha stated her piece, Jesus stated His, and Mary stated hers. Visually, it is stunning to me.

Fill in the blanks of with the sisters' words (We've said it too). First, write Martha's words, then Jesus's words, and then Mary's words.

"_____" ——————-> I AM <———————-——— "_____"

Where is Jesus in this visual? He is in the center!

Read Psalm 46:1, what does it say?

_____

_____

_____

_____

It does not matter where you are at in your story, whether the worst is threatening to happen to you or has already happened. Jesus is still God, and He is right in the center of it all. You may say, "God, had you been here." In John 11:25, Jesus is saying back, "I am."

Whatever and wherever you need Him to be, He already is.

Take time to pray and ask God to show you the way that He was present in the midst of your hurt and loss. Ask God to bring His Word to your heart and mind. It will remind you of who He is.

The Message (MSG)

The Death of Lazarus

A man was sick, Lazarus of Bethany, the town of Mary and her sister Martha. This was the same Mary who massaged the Lord's feet with aromatic oils and then wiped them with her hair. It was her brother Lazarus who was sick. So the sisters sent word to Jesus, "Master, the one you love so very much is sick." When Jesus got the message, he said, "This sickness is not fatal. It will become an occasion to show God's glory by glorifying God's Son." Jesus loved Martha and her sister and Lazarus, but oddly, when he heard that Lazarus was sick, he stayed on where he was for two more days. After the two days, he said to his disciples, "Let's go back to Judea." They said, "Rabbi, you can't do that. The Jews are out to kill you, and you're going back?" Jesus replied, "Are there not twelve hours of daylight? Anyone who walks in daylight doesn't stumble because there's plenty of light from the sun. Walking at night, he might very well stumble because he can't see where he's going." He said these things, and then announced, "Our friend Lazarus has fallen asleep. I'm going to wake him up." The disciples said, "Master, if he's gone to sleep, he'll get a good rest and wake up feeling fine." Jesus was talking about death, while his disciples thought he was talking about taking a nap. Then Jesus became explicit: "Lazarus died. And I am glad for your sakes that I wasn't there. You're about to be given new grounds for believing. Now let's go to him." That's when Thomas, the one called the Twin, said to his companions, "Come along. We might as well die with him." When Jesus finally got there, he found Lazarus already four days dead. Bethany was near Jerusalem, only a couple of miles away, and many of the Jews were visiting Martha and Mary, sympathizing with them over their brother. Martha heard Jesus was coming and went out to meet him. Mary remained in the house. Martha said, "Master, if you'd been here, my brother wouldn't have died. Even now, I know that whatever you ask God he will give you." Jesus said, "Your brother will be raised up." Martha replied, "I know that he will be raised up in the resurrection at the end of time." "You don't have to wait for the End. I am, right now, Resurrection and Life. The one who believes in me, even though he or she dies, will live. And everyone who lives believing in me does not ultimately die at all. Do you believe this?" "Yes, Master. All along I have believed that you are the Messiah, the Son of God who comes into the world." After saying this, she went to her sister Mary and whispered in her ear, "The Teacher is here and is asking for you." The moment she heard that, she jumped up and ran out to him. Jesus had not yet entered the town but was still at the place where Martha had met him. When her sympathizing Jewish friends saw Mary run off, they followed her, thinking she was on her way to the tomb to weep there. Mary came to where Jesus was waiting and fell at his feet, saying, "Master, if only you had been here, my brother would not have died." When Jesus saw her sobbing and the Jews with her sobbing, a deep anger welled up within him. He said, "Where did you put him?" "Master, come and see," they said. Now Jesus wept. The Jews said, "Look how deeply he loved him." Others among them said, "Well, if he loved him so much, why didn't he do something to keep him from dying? After all, he opened the eyes of a blind man." Then Jesus, the anger again welling up within him, arrived at the tomb. It was a simple cave in the hillside with a slab of stone laid against it. Jesus said, "Remove the stone." The sister of the dead man, Martha, said, "Master, by this time there's a stench. He's been dead four days!" Jesus looked her in the eye. "Didn't I tell you that if you believed, you would see the glory of God?" Then, to the others, "Go ahead, take away the stone." They removed the stone. Jesus raised his eyes to heaven and prayed, "Father, I'm grateful that you have listened to me. I know you always do listen, but on account of this crowd standing here I've spoken so that they might believe that you sent me." Then he shouted, "Lazarus, come out!" And he came out, a cadaver, wrapped from head to toe, and with a kerchief over his face. Jesus told them, "Unwrap him and let him loose." (John 11:1–44)

DAY 2

SOLID BELIEF

Ask the Holy Spirit to give you ears to hear, eyes to see, and a heart that is open to His Word. Read Martha's response in Luke 10:38–42.

One of the most striking things about this passage is the way that Jesus responded to both women. Martha is jabbed a lot for her response, the first time we see Mary, Jesus, and her together. But if we are honest, it's easy to see both sides of the story.

Martha just wanted a little help getting things ready so that everyone could sit back and relax when the dinner began. Everyone works hard so that everyone can play hard, right? That's sweet in theory, but those of us with bents toward perfection know that once the night gets started, the distractions don't stop—they ramp up! We ask ourselves a million worrying questions every five minutes. We can drive ourselves up a wall.

Jesus knows this, my friend, and that is why I can imagine Jesus's response to Martha's exasperation as a gentle, "Hey, Martha, come sit a while. Mary is just taking in what won't be offered forever. Come join us, I'd love to share this with you too" (see Luke 10:41–42; paraphrase mine). He wasn't condescending. He wasn't sassy right back to her. He was what He always is: kind.

Now, read John 11:17–27. This woman is always on the lookout. What did Martha do in verse 20? What was her reaction?

_____

_____

_____

_____

It says, "When Martha *heard* Jesus was coming, she went out to meet him" (emphasis mine). Martha didn't have to see Him. He didn't have to call her name. She just had to hear someone mention that He was on the way, and she immediately left to go and meet Him.

When she got to Jesus, she didn't hold back. In our English translations, it says that Martha called Jesus, "Lord," but when you read it in the Greek language, she used the word *kurios*. Let's look at what this word means.

Kurios

Underline the titles you see in the definition.

1. He to whom a person or thing belongs, about which he has power of deciding; master, lord
2. The possessor and disposer of a thing
3. The owner; one who has control of the person, the master
4. In the state: the sovereign, prince, chief, the Roman emperor
5. Is a title of honour expressive of respect and reverence, with which servants greet their master
6. This title is given to: God, the Messiah [22]

Martha was not only showing respect by calling Him Lord but also was calling Jesus royalty. In two sentences, she showed her faith and theology. She was resolved, and she solidly believed that Jesus was Lord, so she declared it!

Read John 11:21–27 again. What would you be feeling if you were in Martha's position?

_____

_____

_____

_____

Martha was probably feeling a range of emotions. She was sad that Jesus didn't show up on time. She was angry that He seemed not to care enough to come when He had been asked. She felt hurt and as if He did not love her family as she thought He had. She was hopeful that He was there now and that He had access to God the Father to give Him whatever He asked for.

This is the reason that feelings always have to be followers and truth always has to lead.

Feelings are helpful. Feelings are good. God welcomes us bringing every emotion to Him. He created them. We don't scare God when we bring our feelings and emotions to Him.

Martha may have felt all these conflicting emotions, but she did not hold God accountable to her feelings. She held God accountable to God. She had no problem telling Jesus the truth.

> If you had been here, my brother would not have died. *But I know* that *even now* God will give you whatever you ask. (Luke 11:21, emphasis mine)

Her statements were true. They were faith-filled statements. Martha knew her theology. She went on to explain that even though her brother was dead, she knew that he would rise in the last resurrection.

Notice this. Jesus revealed one of His great "I Am" declarations. Jesus's use of the words had the same meaning when God said, "I Am," in Exodus 3:14. Jesus was saying that He was God[23].

What did Jesus say about Himself in John 11:25–26?

_____

_____

_____

_____

What question did Jesus ask Martha at the end of verse 26?

_____

_____

_____

_____

"Do you *believe* this?" (emphasis mine). Jesus did not ask her how it made her feel or what she thought about it. No, Jesus was asking Martha what she knew to be true. Martha answers with a great, honest, and true confession.

Look at verse 27 and fill in the blanks.

> I _____ that you _____ the Christ, the Son of _____, who was to _____ to the world.

Robert Mounce observed,

> Even though Lazarus lies dead in the grave, her confidence in who Jesus is and what he can do is not diminished even the slightest. Sorrow fills her heart because her brother is dead, but faith reigns supreme in her confidence that, with Jesus at hand, all is well … her ringing testimony to her conviction that Jesus is the Christ, the Son of God, is a clear indication of her perceptive mind and believing heart.[24]

Martha believed that Jesus was who He said He was.

> Jesus,
>
> The always-busy Martha did not even need a second to think about whether or not she should run out to meet You, her Savior. She responded immediately to the news that You were coming her way.
>
> This is a huge lesson to me. Whatever my loss may look like in my grief, my real, nonstop emotions, or my distractions that I busy myself with, I have a choice to respond the second that I know You are coming. When the Holy Spirit brings to mind any words of comfort, thought of Your compassion, or expression of the Father's great love for me, it is my chance to leave my place of mourning and run to You with my hurts and hopes in tow. I must lead with my confession that You are God, and You *are* good.

American Standard Bible (ASV)

The Death and Resurrection of Lazarus

Now a certain man was sick, Lazarus of Bethany, the village of Mary and her sister Martha. It was the Mary who anointed the Lord with ointment, and wiped His feet with her hair, whose brother Lazarus was sick. So the sisters sent word to Him, saying, "Lord, behold, he whom You love is sick." But when Jesus heard this, He said, "This sickness is not to end in death, but for the glory of God, so that the Son of God may be glorified by it." Now Jesus loved Martha and her sister and Lazarus. So when He heard that he was sick, He then stayed two days longer in the place where He was. Then after this He said to the disciples, "Let us go to Judea again." The disciples said to Him, "Rabbi, the Jews were just now seeking to stone You, and are You going there again?" Jesus answered, "Are there not twelve hours in the day? If anyone walks in the day, he does not stumble, because he sees the light of this world. But if anyone walks in the night, he stumbles, because the light is not in him." This He said, and after that He said to them, "Our friend Lazarus has fallen asleep; but I go, so that I may awaken him out of sleep." The disciples then said to Him, "Lord, if he has fallen asleep, he will recover." Now Jesus had spoken of his death, but they thought that He was speaking of literal sleep. So Jesus then said to them plainly, "Lazarus is dead, and I am glad for your sakes that I was not there, so that you may believe; but let us go to him." Therefore Thomas, who is called Didymus, said to his fellow disciples, "Let us also go, so that we may die with Him." So when Jesus came, He found that he had already been in the tomb four days. Now Bethany was near Jerusalem, about two miles off; and many of the Jews had come to Martha and Mary, to console them concerning their brother. Martha therefore, when she heard that Jesus was coming, went to meet Him, but Mary stayed at the house. Martha then said to Jesus, "Lord, if You had been here, my brother would not have died. Even now I know that whatever You ask of God, God will give You." Jesus said to her, "Your brother will rise again." Martha said to Him, "I know that he will rise again in the resurrection on the last day." Jesus said to her, "I am the resurrection and the life; he who believes in Me will live even if he dies, and everyone who lives and believes in Me will never die. Do you believe this?" She said to Him, "Yes, Lord; I have believed that You are the Christ, the Son of God, even He who comes into the world." When she had said this, she went away and called Mary her sister, saying secretly, "The Teacher is here and is calling for you." And when she heard it, she got up quickly and was coming to Him. Now Jesus had not yet come into the village, but was still in the place where Martha met Him. Then the Jews who were with her in the house, and consoling her, when they saw that Mary got up quickly and went out, they followed her, supposing that she was going to the tomb to weep there. Therefore, when Mary came where Jesus was, she saw Him, and fell at His feet, saying to Him, "Lord, if You had been here, my brother would not have died." When Jesus therefore saw her weeping, and the Jews who came with her also weeping, He was deeply moved in spirit and was troubled, and said, "Where have you laid him?" They said to Him, "Lord, come and see." Jesus wept. So the Jews were saying, "See how He loved him!" But some of them said, "Could not this man, who opened the eyes of the blind man, have kept this man also from dying?" So Jesus, again being deeply moved within, came to the tomb. Now it was a cave, and a stone was lying against it. Jesus said, "Remove the stone." Martha, the sister of the deceased, said to Him, "Lord, by this time there will be a stench, for he has been dead four days." Jesus said to her, "Did I not say to you that if you believe, you will see the glory of God?" So they removed the stone. Then Jesus raised His eyes, and said, "Father, I thank You that You have heard Me. I knew that You always hear Me; but because of the people standing around I said it, so that they may believe that You sent Me." When He had said these things, He cried out with a loud voice, "Lazarus, come forth." The man who had died came forth, bound hand and foot with wrappings, and his face was wrapped around with a cloth. Jesus said to them, "Unbind him, and let him go." (John 11:1–44)

DAY 3

WILLING BELIEF

Ask the Holy Spirit to give you ears to hear, eyes to see, and a heart that is open to His Word. Read John 11:1–44 in the text that is provided. Today we are going to look at Mary's response. Just like we all have some Martha in us, we probably have some Mary too. Mary seemed to be the one that saw the bigger picture, and she wasn't afraid to take the time to take everything in.

Read Luke 10:38–42 again. This time, record Mary's actions.

_____

_____

_____

_____

Next, read John 12:2–8. In the three passages, what stands out about Mary?

_____

_____

_____

_____

Don't mistake being fully present and focused for a lack of personal awareness.

When Jesus visited their home, Mary took the seat at Jesus's feet instead of helping with the preparations. She openly washed His feet with expensive perfume and dried them with her hair while others awkwardly watched in judgment of such an act. But she also ran to those feet when He asked to speak with her.

Just like her sister, her response was immediate, and her belief in God was the same. Martha simply pulled Mary aside and whispered in her ear that Jesus was asking for her, and Mary was out the door—gone! In fact, she left so quickly that the mourning crowd, which customarily gathered with the family, thought that overcome with grief, she was returning to the tomb and that she needed to mourn there. She confessed what she knew was true just as Martha did.

What did Mary say to Jesus in John 11:32?

_____

_____

_____

_____

It only took one name, and she responded. The name of Jesus entered her ears, and her body followed to the place that her soul had always chosen to reside: at the feet of Jesus.

The name of Jesus changes everything. Jesus brings hope. Jesus has authority. Jesus is life.

There's a reason that we pray in Jesus's name. There's a reason that we claim promises of scripture over our circumstances in Jesus's name. Have you ever thought about that? It's easy to get into the habit of saying it and not realizing the significance behind it. It's because His name, Jesus, is the only name that has supreme authorship and authority over *all* things.

Read Philippians 2:9–11, Colossians 1:15–18, and Hebrews 1:1–4 and write down insights about the person that Jesus is, the things that He has done and continues to do, and what our response should be.

_____

_____

_____

_____

What does Jesus state at least five times in the Gospel of John? (See John 14:13–14; 15:16; 16:23–24, 26)

_____

_____

_____

_____

They are not magical words. Just because you use them at the end of a prayer doesn't mean that you will get exactly what you prayed for. By the same token, praying and not using that phrase at the end won't negate the entire prayer—no way. Our God is not as fickle as that.

Jesus is calling our hearts to align with the Father, and in doing so, our wills change from our own to our God's will. The whole goal is to bring glory to God. When we lay down our wills and desire God's will for our lives in the power of Jesus's name, we are transformed for our good, and God gets the glory.

Aren't you glad that we have a name that keeps us from being overcome by this world or evil? My name won't do it, and your name won't either. The greatest, kindest, and strongest person on the planet won't be able to withstand the attacks that the enemy has for us. But as we are covered in the blood of the Lamb and in the Name above all Names, not even a dent will be made in the perfect covering of Christ. Will there be pressure? Sure. Will there be pain? Absolutely. Will there be bruising, scars, and even death? Yes, all those things are coming. But not even a dent will be made in our peace, salvation, and hope of glory.

Mary took those things in. She was able to recognize when something was a major moment. Mary sat at Jesus's feet and listened to all His teachings because she knew that at some point, she wouldn't have the opportunity to sit and listen any longer. She was choosing to believe everything that Jesus said and did. When she broke the perfume over His feet and wiped them with her hair, it was because she knew that He wouldn't be there in the flesh forever. She wanted Him to know how much she loved Him. Jesus even said that she had preemptively anointed His body for burial.

Read John 12:1–7. How did Judas Iscariot react to Mary?

_____

_____

_____

_____

I love that Jesus stood up for her. I love that a good, strong, and authoritative voice of someone, who was protecting the innocent from judgment, said, "Leave her alone." Jesus does that all the time. There will come a point, when facing the enemy and while waiting, when Jesus will say back to him, "Leave her alone."

Yes, He has lessons for you, but rest assured, He is always standing up for you. God is a good Father who loves His children. That does not mean that you will have a perfect, happy, all-is-sunshine life. He allows pain, waiting, and hurtful circumstances because those things have to happen for our good.

Often, it takes time for us to see the good in them. In the most unthinkable turn of events, do not be surprised if down the road, you actually become thankful for it. Do not let the enemy make you bitter or resentful. Take up your God-given armor and start fighting back with the Spirit that is within you.

When Mary ran out to meet Jesus, she threw herself at His feet. Three times, Mary and Jesus's feet are mentioned together. Being at the feet of someone shows humility and devotion. It shows a willingness to learn. It also shows submission to authority. Mary listened, submitted, and sacrificed there.

Read Matthew 26:13 or Mark 14:9. The same story of Mary is in both of them. The last verse is precious.

> Lord,
>
> Let me also live in such a way that when the gospel is shared through my sacrifices and waiting, I will be remembered, not for my sake but for the display of Your grace. In Jesus's name, amen

New Living Translation (NLT)

The Raising of Lazarus

A man named Lazarus was sick. He lived in Bethany with his sisters, Mary and Martha. This is the Mary who later poured the expensive perfume on the Lord's feet and wiped them with her hair. Her brother, Lazarus, was sick. So the two sisters sent a message to Jesus telling him, "Lord, your dear friend is very sick." But when Jesus heard about it he said, "Lazarus's sickness will not end in death. No, it happened for the glory of God so that the Son of God will receive glory from this." So although Jesus loved Martha, Mary, and Lazarus, he stayed where he was for the next two days. Finally, he said to his disciples, "Let's go back to Judea." But his disciples objected. "Rabbi," they said, "only a few days ago the people in Judea were trying to stone you. Are you going there again?" Jesus replied, "There are twelve hours of daylight every day. During the day people can walk safely. They can see because they have the light of this world. But at night there is danger of stumbling because they have no light." Then he said, "Our friend Lazarus has fallen asleep, but now I will go and wake him up." The disciples said, "Lord, if he is sleeping, he will soon get better!" They thought Jesus meant Lazarus was simply sleeping, but Jesus meant Lazarus had died. So he told them plainly, "Lazarus is dead. And for your sakes, I'm glad I wasn't there, for now you will really believe. Come, let's go see him." Thomas, nicknamed the Twin, said to his fellow disciples, "Let's go, too—and die with Jesus." When Jesus arrived at Bethany, he was told that Lazarus had already been in his grave for four days. Bethany was only a few miles down the road from Jerusalem, and many of the people had come to console Martha and Mary in their loss. When Martha got word that Jesus was coming, she went to meet him. But Mary stayed in the house. Martha said to Jesus, "Lord, if only you had been here, my brother would not have died. But even now I know that God will give you whatever you ask." Jesus told her, "Your brother will rise again." "Yes," Martha said, "he will rise when everyone else rises, at the last day." Jesus told her, "I am the resurrection and the life. Anyone who believes in me will live, even after dying. Everyone who lives in me and believes in me will never ever die. Do you believe this, Martha?" "Yes, Lord," she told him. "I have always believed you are the Messiah, the Son of God, the one who has come into the world from God." Then she returned to Mary. She called Mary aside from the mourners and told her, "The Teacher is here and wants to see you." So Mary immediately went to him. Jesus had stayed outside the village, at the place where Martha met him. When the people who were at the house consoling Mary saw her leave so hastily, they assumed she was going to Lazarus's grave to weep. So they followed her there. When Mary arrived and saw Jesus, she fell at his feet and said, "Lord, if only you had been here, my brother would not have died." When Jesus saw her weeping and saw the other people wailing with her, a deep anger welled up within him, and he was deeply troubled. "Where have you put him?" he asked them. They told him, "Lord, come and see." Then Jesus wept. The people who were standing nearby said, "See how much he loved him!" But some said, "This man healed a blind man. Couldn't he have kept Lazarus from dying?" Jesus was still angry as he arrived at the tomb, a cave with a stone rolled across its entrance. "Roll the stone aside," Jesus told them. But Martha, the dead man's sister, protested, "Lord, he has been dead for four days. The smell will be terrible." Jesus responded, "Didn't I tell you that you would see God's glory if you believe?" So they rolled the stone aside. Then Jesus looked up to heaven and said, "Father, thank you for hearing me. You always hear me, but I said it out loud for the sake of all these people standing here, so that they will believe you sent me." Then Jesus shouted, "Lazarus, come out!" And the dead man came out, his hands and feet bound in graveclothes, his face wrapped in a headcloth. Jesus told them, "Unwrap him and let him go!" (John 11:1–44)

DAY 4

EVIDENT BELIEF

Ask the Holy Spirit to give you ears to hear, eyes to see, and a heart that is open to His Word. Read John 11:1–44 in the text that is provided. Focus on John 11:33–36.

I don't know about you, but I need the God who can move mountains, part seas, and perform miracles. But I also need the God who has the ability to hurt with me and be tender. This does not take away His Power. In fact, I believe it highlights it! Our God is moved with compassion. No other god is because there is no other God.

What do the following verses say about God's response to our cries?

Psalm 10:17

_____

_____

_____

_____

Psalm 18:6

_____

_____

_____

_____

Psalm 34:6

_____

_____

_____

_____

Psalm 34:15, 17

_____

_____

_____

_____

Psalm 56:8–9

_____

_____

_____

_____

> *Where we have made religion into striving to do our best, Jesus*
> *offers a relationship where He will sit with you and let you rest your*
> *head as He bottles every tear from your eyes. That is our God.*

But while Jesus can be moved with compassion, we have to remember that it is not only about us. God does hear our cries and prayers, and He acts on them. I always thought that "Jesus wept" meant that He felt bad that the sisters were having to go through those things, but oddly enough, it is not the point of John 11:35. Let the *Expositor's Bible Commentary* open your eyes.

> The reason for Jesus' tears in the Lazarus story was not grief over Lazarus's death—that would bracket him with those "who have no hope" (1 Th 4:13). Nor was it simply an expression of love and concern for the sisters and their friends. Jesus wept because of the havoc wrought on the world by sin and death. To the

one who came to bring life, death was a stark reminder of the continuing cosmic struggle between God and Satan for the souls of men and women. As long as death reigned, the kingdom of God was not yet finally and completely established.

The Jews failed to understand the real cause of Jesus' tears. They said, "See how he loved him!"—an observation true enough, but one that fell far short of the real reason for Jesus' tears. He wept over the sad state of a people too blind to see that in him there is life eternal and that by faith in him death is transformed into a gateway to eternal bliss. It was the tragic state of their spiritual blindness that caused him pain and brought tears to his eyes.[25]

I'm sorry if that bursts your bubble, but let it actually sink into your heart. Jesus was weeping because people were lost and blind. They couldn't see that their salvation was right in front of them. Mary and Martha understood it. It was completely evident to them. They fully believed that Jesus could raise Lazarus from the dead, but many, who were around them, missed the fact that Jesus was the resurrection. However, Mary and Martha would find out that their wait would be well worth it.

Have you ever experienced a time when it seemed like God kept you from doing something that you really wanted to pursue, but as time unfolded, there ended up being a reason that He hadn't let it come to pass at that time?

_____

_____

_____

_____

Read 2 Peter 3:9. How does this correlate with John 11:17–44?

_____

_____

_____

_____

There is always greater glory at stake. Although our waiting can feel intensely personal, it can serve a greater purpose and bring God glory. Ask the Lord to show you how your waiting will be used for good in the lives of others.

If it seems unfair that you should have to suffer so that others can be set free, ask God to tenderly hold your heart. Confess your frustration but also ask Him to soften your heart so that you can have a willingness to meet others in places that you have been and where they feel alone.

New King James Version (NKJV)

The Death of Lazarus

Now a certain man was sick, Lazarus of Bethany, the town of Mary and her sister Martha. It was that Mary who anointed the Lord with fragrant oil and wiped His feet with her hair, whose brother Lazarus was sick. Therefore the sisters sent to Him, saying, "Lord, behold, he whom You love is sick." When Jesus heard that, He said, "This sickness is not unto death, but for the glory of God, that the Son of God may be glorified through it." Now Jesus loved Martha and her sister and Lazarus. So, when He heard that he was sick, He stayed two more days in the place where He was. Then after this He said to the disciples, "Let us go to Judea again." The disciples said to Him, "Rabbi, lately the Jews sought to stone You, and are You going there again?" Jesus answered, "Are there not twelve hours in the day? If anyone walks in the day, he does not stumble, because he sees the light of this world. But if one walks in the night, he stumbles, because the light is not in him." These things He said, and after that He said to them, "Our friend Lazarus sleeps, but I go that I may wake him up." Then His disciples said, "Lord, if he sleeps he will get well." However, Jesus spoke of his death, but they thought that He was speaking about taking rest in sleep. Then Jesus said to them plainly, "Lazarus is dead. And I am glad for your sakes that I was not there, that you may believe. Nevertheless let us go to him." Then Thomas, who is called the Twin, said to his fellow disciples, "Let us also go, that we may die with Him."

I Am the Resurrection and the Life

So when Jesus came, He found that he had already been in the tomb four days. Now Bethany was near Jerusalem, about two miles away. And many of the Jews had joined the women around Martha and Mary, to comfort them concerning their brother. Then Martha, as soon as she heard that Jesus was coming, went and met Him, but Mary was sitting in the house. Now Martha said to Jesus, "Lord, if You had been here, my brother would not have died. But even now I know that whatever You ask of God, God will give You." Jesus said to her, "Your brother will rise again." Martha said to Him, "I know that he will rise again in the resurrection at the last day." Jesus said to her, "I am the resurrection and the life. He who believes in Me, though he may die, he shall live. And whoever lives and believes in Me shall never die. Do you believe this?" She said to Him, "Yes, Lord, I believe that You are the Christ, the Son of God, who is to come into the world."

Jesus and Death, the Last Enemy

And when she had said these things, she went her way and secretly called Mary her sister, saying, "The Teacher has come and is calling for you." As soon as she heard that, she arose quickly and came to Him. Now Jesus had not yet come into the town, but was in the place where Martha met Him. Then the Jews who were with her in the house, and comforting her, when they saw that Mary rose up quickly and went out, followed her, saying, "She is going to the tomb to weep there." Then, when Mary came where Jesus was, and saw Him, she fell down at His feet, saying to Him, "Lord, if You had been here, my brother would not have died." Therefore, when Jesus saw her weeping, and the Jews who came with her weeping, He groaned in the spirit and was troubled. And He said, "Where have you laid him?" They said to Him, "Lord, come and see." Jesus wept. Then the Jews said, "See how He loved him!" And some of them said, "Could not this Man, who opened the eyes of the blind, also have kept this man from dying?"

Lazarus Raised from the Dead

Then Jesus, again groaning in Himself, came to the tomb. It was a cave, and a stone lay against it. Jesus said, "Take away the stone." Martha, the sister of him who was dead, said to Him, "Lord, by this time there is a stench, for he has been dead four days." Jesus said to her, "Did I not say to you that if you would believe you would see the glory of God?" Then they took away the stone from the place where the dead man was lying. And Jesus lifted up His eyes and said, "Father, I thank You that You have heard Me. And I know that You always hear Me, but because of the people who are standing by I said this, that they may believe that You sent Me." Now when He had said these things, He cried with a loud voice, "Lazarus, come forth!" And he who had died came out bound hand and foot with graveclothes, and his face was wrapped with a cloth. Jesus said to them, "Loose him, and let him go." (John 11:1–44)

DAY 5

POWERFUL BELIEF

Ask the Holy Spirit to give you ears to hear, eyes to see, and a heart that is open to His Word. Read John 11:1–44 in the text that is provided.

Four days passed for Mary and Martha, in what should have been a short journey for their Lord to travel and heal their brother. In ancient Jewish custom, it was believed that the soul would hover over a body for three days and re-enter the body if it desired, but once the person's face started to change, the soul would leave permanently. So consequently on day four, there was no question that Lazarus was dead and past the point of resuscitation. He would need a miracle of resurrection.[26]

The sisters probably felt confused and abandoned by the One who could actually do something to help their brother but had instead chose to arrive, by all human accounts, late to the scene. But on His arrival, Jesus was on the verge of causing a massive outbreak of worship and bringing people from death to life spiritually (see John 11:17, 45).

Again, only at the appointed time will God do His greatest work. The response is always worship.

So what was the spiritual benefit from Mary and Martha's experience? It was a display of God's glory. If they had not had to wait, they would have been thankful that their brother had been saved, but they would not have seen Jesus do the impossible and raise their eyes and hearts to behold the glory of their Father.

Jesus said, "Did I not tell you that if you believed, you would see the glory of God?"(John 11:40). According to Mark Bailey and Tom Constable, "Sometimes the Lord delays His answers to prayer to show more of His glory through much greater works."[27] It was never *only* for the benefit of Mary and Martha. It was for the whole assembly of mourners and for us today. God used their waiting and circumstances to bring a crowd to mourn with them so that many more people would see God's display and believe.[28] Over two thousand years later, we read about it and are in awe as well.

Do you know who else experienced an appointed time with Jesus and left His presence worshipping? The Samaritan woman at the well, who is found in John 4:1–29, 39–42, also experienced it. You're already close to it. Just flip back a few pages and read it for yourself.

We could unpack much here. A man was talking to a woman, a Jew was talking to a Samaritan, and a pure person was interacting with an unclean person. It's beautiful the way Jesus always sees a heart and goes after it.

Because other women in the community looked down on her, she had to wait. She had to wait to go draw water from the well in the heat of the day. Can you imagine the internal mental and emotional anguish she experienced every day? But her waiting brought her into direct contact with her Savior.

Does Jesus shame the woman for her lifestyle? (verse 17)

_____

_____

_____

_____

What does Jesus reveal about Himself to her? (verses 24 and 26)

_____

_____

_____

_____

How should she worship? (verse 24)

_____

_____

_____

_____

What was her response to Jesus? (verses 28–29)

_____

_____

_____

_____

What was the result of her worship? (verses 39–42)

_____

_____

_____

_____

Just like Mary and Martha, her wait and the person that she encountered in it were not only for her own benefit. They all worshipped and through their powerful belief that Jesus is who He says He is, so many others not only joined in in worship as well, but they placed their faith and trust in Jesus too.

Pay attention to each response from Mary and Martha. They both were quick to move toward Jesus. In the times of deepest hurt when Jesus seems far off or He calls His child by name, the response is to always come to Him quickly. In doing so, He will meet the greatest need with the greatest personal affection toward those who come quickly. His joy and delight is to walk and mourn with you, yet He wants to bring glory to His Father at the same time.

How do you need to adjust the way that you respond to loss? To waiting?

_____

_____

_____

_____

Read Titus 2:13 and remember what we are ultimately waiting for and what He represents.

_____

_____

_____

_____

Lord,

I thank You for the six women in this study and the truth that they spoke into my own waiting. Keep Your truth fresh in my mind, even after this study ends. Help me to never forsake what You have purposed for me. Thank You for this season of waiting. Thank You for the good that will come out of it.

FINAL THOUGHTS

Through the examples of Sarah, Hannah, Mary (the mother of Jesus), Anna, Mary, and Martha, God has given us clear examples of the many benefits that come to our spiritual lives in the seasons of waiting. Waiting is often painful and seldom enjoyable, but the depths to which God will take our relationship with Him during those times, are beyond any place that we knew could exist prior to those seasons.

It shows us our utter dependence on Him. It exposes what we truly believe in our hearts about Him and what are motives are toward Him. During that time if we choose to trust Him, He seals in us an overwhelming sense of peace in His sovereignty over our circumstances. Although we would like to learn these lessons a different, more convenient, and less heartbreaking way, the truth is that we would not have the level of trust in God, flourishing prayer lives, or intimate times with Him, if we did not walk through the harshness of winter in order to get to the harvest of autumn.

The Bible leaves little doubt about whom we can trust in our waiting and gives us glimpses of the purpose behind it.

> The Lord will perfect that which concerns me. Thy mercy, Oh Lord, endures forever; Do not forsake the works of your hands.[29]

Often, the wait is preparing us for the result. God will not forsake the works of His hands. He is concerned with everything that we encounter in our lives, and He will perfect it. But that takes time, which is why He reminds us that His love and mercy endure forever. If we did not have to wait, we would not be ready to handle what we were waiting for.

Further, the writers in Psalms claim, "Those who look to the Lord are radiant, their faces are never covered in shame" (Psalm 34:5). Multiple times, they remind us that it is right to wait on the Lord and that He hears our cries (see Psalms 5:3; 27:14; 33:20–22; 40:1).

Because waiting has to do with a measure of time, it is important to see in each example that an appointed time was stated. Sarah bore a son "at the very time God had promised him" (Genesis 21:2). For Hannah, "in the course of time she conceived and gave birth to a son" (1 Samuel 1:20). For Mary, "the time came for the baby to be born" (Luke 2:5). Anna was *"coming up to them at that very moment"* to see the face of redemption (Luke 2:38). Mary and Martha experienced a life-changing event "on His arrival." (John 11:17).

This allows us to boldly believe that God has an appointed time for our waiting to end. We present-day believers wait for the return of our Lord and Savior, Jesus Christ. We fully trust and believe that there is a specific time and place that this will take place. We do not know when, but we have full confidence that it will be at just the right time and that God will appoint it.

Another spiritual benefit in the examples that have been given is the inseparable combination of worship and prayer. In our seasons of waiting, it would serve us well to recognize that the way to thrive rather than survive is to devotedly understand that we have been given weapons against bitterness, anxiety, and anger through prayer and worship. As believers, we are allowed to plead with God. We bring all our longings before Him, just as we are to worship Him at all times regardless of our situations (Psalms 34:1; 38:9).

Ultimately, it is for God's glory. It is to point others to Jesus. While we get to reap the benefits of peace and a deepening relationship with God, others get to experience the Holy Spirit changing their own hearts as they watch our lives of faith while we wait. Jesus said that in our times of waiting, "It is for God's glory so that God's Son may be glorified through it." (John 11:4). The goal of our lives is to love God and glorify Him.

I love how Tomas Halik puts it.

> To love God means being profoundly grateful for the miracle of life and expressing gratitude through my life, assenting to my fate, even when it eludes my plans and expectations. To love God means accepting human encounters patiently and attentively as meaningful messages from God, even when I am unable to properly understand them. To love God means to trust that even the most difficult and darkest moments will one day reveal their meaning to me, so that I will be able to say to them, "God was in there? Well then, once more!"[30]

Whether the situation is impossible as Sarah's was, insulting as Hannah's was, unknown as Mary's was, living in a culture of upheaval toward the things of God like Anna's was, or at a time of immense loss like Mary and Martha's was, was God in it? Yes. Our response simply becomes, "Well then, once more!"

DISCUSSION QUESTIONS

Week 1

1. Have you experienced an impossible circumstance that you would be willing to share?
2. Reread 2 Corinthians 4:18. How does this comfort you in your situation? Do you know what "the unseen" is concerning it?
3. With the focus being on hope this week, how has Sarah's story increased your hope?

Week 2

1. Think deeply about the impact of words. How have they helped or hindered your decisions, perspectives, and responses throughout your life?
2. Do you sometimes pull back from God because you think you will hurt or offend Him or that He cannot handle your thoughts?
3. What can we learn from Hannah as far as words go? What do her words say about her belief in God's view of her honesty? What about her faith? What about her response?

Week 3

1. What was the last unknown that you faced? Did it make you fearful? Did you feel confused? Did you have a hard time accepting it?
2. Do you tend to focus more on the known or the unknown? Why?
3. Faith cost Mary something. That does not mean it was not worth it. How much has faith cost you?

Week 4

1. Without getting political, discuss the upheaval being experienced around the world, your country, your city, and your home.
2. In what ways do you need to let God manage your mindset? What are the benefits of letting God take over?
3. Anna's mindset prepared her to see God at work. What is your mindset allowing you to see?

Week 5

1. Do you tend to respond more like Mary or Martha? Why?
2. In what ways are you recognizing that Jesus is at the center of your circumstance? (See page 76).
3. God used Mary and Martha's belief to reveal His power and glory to others. What can God use your belief to do?

NOTES

Week 1

Day 2

1. Augustine of Hippo, *The City of God*, in *Saint Augustin's City of God and Christian Doctrine*, ed. Philip Schaff, trans. Marcus Dods, vol. 2, *A Select Library of the Nicene and Post-Nicene Fathers of the Christian Church, First Series* (Buffalo, NY: Christian Literature Company, 1887), 328.

Day 3

2. Hamilton, Victor P. "Abraham" Essay. In Handbook on the Pentateuch: Genesis, Exodus, Leviticus, Numbers, Deuteronomy, (Grand Rapids, MI: Baker Book House, 2015), 90
3. Beth Moore, "Faith According to Romans 4," Audio CD. Living proof Ministries, accessed January 15, 2021, https://store.lproof.org/products/faith-according-to-romans-four.
4. Steven J. Cole, "Lesson 33: Why We Have Family Problems," Bible.org, accessed January 29, 2019, https://bible.org/seriespage/lesson-33-why-we-have-family-problems-genesis-161-6.
5. *Standard Bible Dictionary* (Cincinnati: Standard Publishing, 2006), s.v. "Sarah."

Day 4

6. Chad Brand et al., eds., *Holman Illustrated Bible Dictionary* (Nashville: Holman Bible Publishers, 2003), s.v. "laugh."
7. Allen P. Ross, "Genesis," in *The Bible Knowledge Commentary: An Exposition of the Scriptures*, eds. J. F. Walvoord and R. B. Zuck (Wheaton, IL: Victor Books, 1985).
8. M. Beeching, *New Bible Dictionary*, ed. D. R. W. Wood (Leicester, UK;: InterVarsity Press, 1996), s.v. "Sarah, Sarai."

Day 5

9. "The Patriarchal Period," Biblical Archeology, Truthnet.org, accessed May 30, 2018, http://www.truthnet.org/Biblicalarcheology/2/Patriarchalperiod.htm.

Week 2

Day 2

10. Brown, Driver, Briggs and Gesenius. "Hebrew Lexicon entry for Bakah". "The KJV Old Testament Hebrew Lexicon". Accessed February 20, 2021, https://www.biblestudytools.com/lexicons/hebrew/kjv/bakah.html

Week 3

Day 1

11. Clayton Harrop, "Intertestamental History and Literature," *Holman Illustrated Bible Dictionary*, ed. Chad Brand et al. (Nashville, TN: Holman Bible Publishers, 2003), 830.

Day 2

12. Walter L. Liefeld and David W. Pao, "Luke," in *The Expositor's Bible Commentary: Luke–Acts,* rev. ed., eds. Tremper Longman III and David E. Garland, vol. 10 (Grand Rapids: Zondervan, 2007).

Day 3

13. Walter L. Liefeld and David W. Pao, "Luke," in *The Expositor's Bible Commentary: Luke–Acts*, rev. ed., eds. Tremper Longman III and David E. Garland, vol. 10 (Grand Rapids: Zondervan, 2007), 83.

Day 5

14. Walter L. Liefeld and David W. Pao, "Luke," in *The Expositor's Bible Commentary: Luke–Acts*, rev. ed., eds. Tremper Longman III and David E. Garland, vol. 10 (Grand Rapids: Zondervan, 2007), 61.

Week 4

Day 3

15. *The Lexham Bible Dictionary,* ed. John D. Barry et al. (Bellingham, WA: Lexham Press, 2016), s.v. "Anna the Prophetess."

Day 4

16. Larry Richards and Lawrence O. Richards, *The Teacher's Commentary* (Wheaton, IL: Victor Books, 1987), 511.
17. Thayer and Smith. "Greek Lexicon entry for Lutrosis". "The KJV New Testament Greek Lexicon". accessed January 15, 2021, https://www.biblestudytools.com/lexicons/greek/nas/lutrosis.html
18. Thayer and Smith. "Greek Lexicon entry for Luo". "The KJV New Testament Greek Lexicon". accessed January 15, 2021, https://www.biblestudytools.com/lexicons/greek/nas/luo.html

Day 5

19. Elizabeth Fletcher, "Anna, the Prophetess in Luke's Gospel," Women in the Bible, accessed May 28, 2018, http://www.womeninthebible.net/women-bible-old-new-testaments/anna/.

Week 5

Day 1

20. John F. Walvoord and Roy B. Zuck, *The Bible Knowledge Commentary: An Exposition of the Scriptures* (Wheaton, IL: Victor Books, 1983), 313.
21. Mark Bailey and Tom Constable, *Nelson's New Testament Survey: Discovering the Essence, Background and Meaning about Every New Testament Book* (Nashville: Thomas Nelson, 2009), 179.

Day 2

22. Thayer and Smith. "Greek Lexicon entry for Kurios". "The NAS New Testament Greek Lexicon". Accessed January 15, 2021, https://www.biblestudytools.com/lexicons/greek/nas/kurios.html
23. Allen, Trevor. "The Significance of the 'I AM' statements in the Bible". Accessed January 15,2021, http://www.livingwater-spain.com/iaminbib.pdf

24. Robert H. Mounce, "John," in *The Expositor's Bible Commentary: Luke–Acts,* rev. ed., eds. Tremper Longman III and David E. Garland, vol. 10 (Grand Rapids: Zondervan, 2007).

Day 4

25. Robert H. Mounce, "John," in *The Expositor's Bible Commentary: Luke–Acts,* rev. ed., eds. Tremper Longman III and David E. Garland, vol. 10 (Grand Rapids: Zondervan, 2007).

Day 5

26. Robert H. Mounce, "John," in *The Expositor's Bible Commentary: Luke–Acts,* rev. ed., eds. Tremper Longman III and David E. Garland, vol. 10 (Grand Rapids: Zondervan, 2007).
27. Mark Bailey and Tom Constable, *Nelson's New Testament Survey: Discovering the Essence, Background and Meaning about Every New Testament Book* (Nashville: Thomas Nelson, 2009), 179.
28. Bailey and Constable, *Nelson's New Testament,* 179.

Final Thoughts

29. *The Macarthur Study Bible: New King James Version* (Nashville: Word Bibles, 1997), 865.
30. Tomáš Halík, *I Want You to Be: On the God of Love* (Notre Dame, IN: University of Notre Dame Press, 2016), 106.

Printed in the United States
by Baker & Taylor Publisher Services